"A crucial guide to the class struggle that exists in the home, not just the workplace. *Renoviction and Resistance in the Capitalist City* is an accessible and indispensable handbook on the strength of autonomous tenant organizing and the weakness of relying on legalistic and non-profit approaches."

—Mike Gouldhawke, contributor to *Briarpatch* and the Yellowhead Institute

"During unprecedented displacement driven by the hyper-commodification of housing, *Renoviction and Resistance in the Capitalist City* is an urgent and timely book grounded in the authors' experience as tenant organizers. Webber and Zigman meticulously lay bare the landlords' strategic playbook for expulsion and rent extraction, unequivocally demonstrating that renoviction is not actually about renovations or improving tenants' quality of life. They document powerful examples of effective tenant resistance, proving that while renovictions have proliferated, they are not a foregone conclusion. Tenants can organize, fight back, and ultimately change their landlords' eviction plans."

—Andrew Crosby, Carleton University, author of *Resisting Eviction*

"Webber and Zigman challenge prevailing narrow definitions of renoviction and illustrate how landlords use renovictions as a profit-generating strategy to close rent gaps in 'undermanaged' buildings with low rents. Their incisive book highlights the social impacts of renovictions and the extralegal tactics landlords have employed to displace tenants. Importantly, they also detail strategies and actions tenants have deployed to successfully resist renoviction and remain in their homes."

—Julie Mah, Eviction Research Lab, New Housing Alternatives Partnership, University of Toronto

"*Renoviction and Resistance in the Capitalist City* is essential reading for people who care about radical housing justice. Webber and Zigman offer us a rigorous study of renoviction deeply rooted in organizing wisdom and experience, which exposes mainstream myths about our housing system, and offers an energizing guide for tenants who want to fight displacement and build community power.

—Martine August, associate professor, School of Planning, University of Waterloo

"*Renoviction and Resistance in the Capitalist City* unravels the cover offered to landlords by a legal system and real estate industry that profits from the displacement of tenants from their homes. It lays bare how evictions, both legal and illegal, are about property values and investment income. Policy tweaks masked as 'tenant rights' further entrench evictions as a legitimate tool of property owners. This book clearly explains what motivates renovictions and offers up its best antidote: organized working-class people collectively fighting the concerted efforts to evict them. Its mission is compelling and required reading for tenants and their advocates."

—Samuel Mason, tenant lawyer, Parkdale
Community Legal Services

RENOVICTION AND RESISTANCE IN THE CAPITALIST CITY

Cole Webber and
Philip Zigman

Renoviction and Resistance in the Capitalist City

First published in 2026 by
Between the Lines
401 Richmond Street West, Studio 281
Toronto, Ontario • M5V 3A8 • Canada
www.btlbooks.com

Library and Archives Canada Cataloguing in Publication
Title: Renoviction and resistance in the capitalist city / by Cole Webber and Philip Zigman.
Names: Webber, Cole, author. | Zigman, Philip, author.
Description: Includes bibliographical references.
Identifiers: Canadiana (print) 20260132063 | Canadiana (ebook) 20260132195 | ISBN 9781771136990 (softcover) | ISBN 9781771137003 (EPUB)
Subjects: LCSH: Landlord and tenant. | LCSH: Eviction. | LCSH: Rental housing—Law and legislation.
Classification: LCC HD7288.8 .W43 2026 | DDC 333.33/854—dc23

Cover and Text design by DEEVE

Printed in Canada

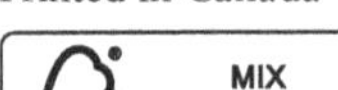

We acknowledge for their financial support of our publishing activities: the Government of Canada; the Canada Council for the Arts; and the Government of Ontario through the Ontario Arts Council, the Ontario Book Publishers Tax Credit program, and Ontario Creates.

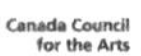

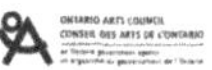

CONTENTS

INTRODUCTION

The term "renoviction" was first picked up by the Canadian news media in 2008, and in a little over a decade renoviction grew into a major topic, albeit a frequently misunderstood one, in discussions about housing across the country.[1] Often accompanied by a short definition or appearing inside quotation marks, renoviction is something of a catchall standing in for a range of landlord practices viewed as predatory.[2] Journalists report on the rise of renovictions and advise tenants on how to protect themselves from being pushed out of their homes.[3] Academics list renovictions as among the main threats to our existing supply of affordable housing.[4] Politicians at the federal, provincial, and municipal levels campaign on the promise to stop renovictions, while some cities have introduced new laws to try to curb them.[5] Non-profits and housing rights organizations, for their part, have supported these reforms and recently celebrated the introduction of renoviction bylaws in Hamilton and Toronto, which some of these organizations will help administer.

In Ontario, renoviction is frequently associated with a specific type of eviction notice, the N13. An N13 is a notice that a landlord can issue to a tenant to terminate their tenancy because the landlord wants to conduct extensive renovations within the rental unit, demolish the unit, or convert it to commercial use; giving a tenant such a notice is the first step in the legal eviction process. If a landlord files an application with the Landlord and Tenant Board (LTB) to evict a tenant on the basis of an N13, then a hearing will be scheduled where an adjudicator will hear the case. If an adjudicator orders an eviction in a case where the landlord is seeking to evict a tenant for extensive renovations, then according to the law, the tenant is able to return to their home at their old rent after the renovations are complete. This is sometimes called "the right of first refusal" or "the right to return." In reality, as we will discuss, this is not something that happens.

This book examines the conditions that give rise to renoviction, the ways landlords go about renovicting tenants, the state's role in enabling and perpetuating renoviction, and the principles guiding tenants who have organized to keep their homes. As organizers living in Toronto, most of our experience with renoviction and with tenants who have fought back against their landlords' attempts to push them out of their homes comes from that city. The book is informed by around two hundred cases of renoviction in Toronto over several years, with each case being a building where renoviction took place or is currently taking place, affecting anywhere from one to seventy or more tenants. We conducted extensive interviews with twenty-five tenants who have experienced renoviction and organized to fight back, from thirteen of these buildings. We also interviewed organizers and one tenant lawyer involved in fights against renoviction in Hamilton, Toronto, Ottawa, Montreal, and Halifax.

One of the difficulties in discussing renoviction is that the data around the practice is so poor. Like with evictions more generally, many renovictions are informal and there is no evidence to be found in the state's own recordkeeping of these cases. For example, in Ontario the government only tracks eviction applications filed by landlords—and even here, the actual outcomes of eviction hearings for these applications is not tracked. There are no systematic data collection efforts documenting when landlords approach tenants about moving out in person or by phone, text, or email, when landlords offer tenants buyouts in exchange for terminating their tenancies, or when landlords give tenants N13 eviction notices for extensive renovations. A project like RenovictionsTO, which relies largely on reports submitted by tenants to document renovictions in Toronto, may help to collect data about how renovictions play out, where many renovictions are happening, which landlords are engaging in the practice, and how tenants respond—but there is no way to know what small share of the total renovictions are being documented, not to mention what biases may exist in the data as a result of how it is collected and the project's very limited publicization efforts. Meanwhile, N13 eviction notices are used by landlords not only to evict tenants for extensive renovations, but when demolishing a building as well. Thus, an increase in eviction applications filed on the basis of N13 eviction notices may indicate an increase in the overall incidence of renoviction (as is sometimes claimed) but could also indicate an increase in demolitions or an increase in tenants who do not simply move out after receiving an N13 notice.[6]

Our objective is not to quantify renovictions or attempt to analyze the incidence of the practice over time. Rather, by drawing on around two hundred cases of renoviction and the experiences of tenants from these buildings, as well as our own first-hand experience with many of these cases, we aim to faithfully describe a landlord practice, how tenants have responded, and the political and economic background against which renoviction takes place. Despite our focus on Toronto, and Ontario more generally, our analysis of renoviction and tenant resistance is informed by cases from across the country and is relevant wherever similar rental market dynamics exist across Canada.

The presentation of this book proceeds as follows. In chapter 1, we define "renoviction" as a specific landlord strategy and argue that renoviction is primarily about displacement, not renovations. We show that while the particular rules surrounding evictions and rent increases vary somewhat from province to province, Canadian landlords renovict tenants not to rehabilitate aging rental housing stock, but rather to close the gap between actual and potential rents. We compare renoviction with other landlord strategies for closing rent gaps to demonstrate that renoviction is a distinct practice often employed by certain types of landlords and thus warrants inquiry. Contrary to the claim made by governments and non-profits—based on either misunderstandings of renoviction or attempts to obscure its reality—we argue that a better understanding of the law alone will not protect tenants from renoviction.

Chapter 2 analyzes how renovictions actually play out in buildings and describes the landlord's playbook for renovicting tenants. Here, we detail the legal and extralegal tactics that make up the landlord renoviction strategy. We show that renovictions are dynamic, conflict-ridden situations in which the landlord's approach and commitment level, as well as how tenants respond, determine how the situation develops and culminates.

In chapter 3, we focus on how tenants have organized at their buildings in response to landlords' attempts to remove them from their homes through renoviction. We then present the Keele Area Tenant Committee (KATC) in north Toronto as an example of working-class organizing against renoviction at the level of a renter district. We show that by organizing at their buildings and in their renter districts, tenants have successfully beat renoviction despite having been issued N13 notices and have kept their homes in the face of other renoviction tactics. Through their experiences organizing against renoviction, some tenants have developed their political and ethical commitments, becoming new organizers who have gone on to support other tenants at different buildings in renoviction fights.

Chapter 4 discusses the state's involvement in renoviction, arguing that the state is a political form that maintains the conditions for urban rent extraction. The state creates the conditions that make renoviction possible and profitable and furnishes landlords with the means to counter tenant organizing. As a result of the apparent rise in renovictions and the attention they receive, the state has introduced policies meant to curb the practice. Despite enthusiastic support for these reforms from non-profits and tenant advocates, we argue that policy responses to renoviction actually give the practice new legitimacy and undermine tenant organizing.

For years, the public discussion surrounding renoviction and policy responses such as the development of the new renoviction bylaws in Hamilton and Toronto have obscured the conditions that give rise to renoviction and how landlords go about renovicting tenants. Yet a growing number of tenants have continued to organize against renoviction, demonstrating for others that it is possible to fight back and defend their homes. Successful organizing against renoviction has provided other tenants facing displacement threats with greater clarity about what their landlords are trying to do, what motivates their landlords, and how they would be affected if they were forced out of their homes. As a result, more working-class people are learning to fight back against renoviction and communicating these lessons to tenants as they support new organizing initiatives based in buildings and in renter districts.[7]

ONE

Understanding Renoviction

Discussions of renovictions often characterize them as "illegitimate" or "illegal" cases of eviction where tenants are permanently displaced from their homes. The definition of "renoviction" used by the City of Toronto has changed over time, but the City has consistently defined renovictions as "illegitimate" evictions and instances where landlords do not follow the rules. In November 2019, a City report said the term "refers to instances where landlords illegitimately evict tenants to undertake renovations of properties and do not provide them with the option to return so that the homes can be re-rented at a much higher price to a new tenant."[1] A 2021 report defined renovictions more narrowly, as instances "where a landlord issues a N13 eviction notice to a tenant under the guise of undertaking renovations but does not follow the requirements of the *Residential Tenancies Act*."[2] A 2022 staff report that accompanied a framework for a potential renoviction bylaw noted that "there has been a growing trend of 'renovictions' in Toronto whereby a landlord illegitimately evicts a tenant by alleging that they need vacant possession of a residential unit to undertake renovations or repairs."[3]

Many non-profits also characterize renoviction as "illegal" or as instances where landlords do not follow the rules. For example, when the Alliance to End Homelessness Ottawa asked tenants to report their renoviction, they said their survey was "for anyone who may have experienced an illegal eviction."[4] The Canadian Centre for Housing Rights and National Right to Housing Network put out a renovations guide for tenants, wherein they say that renovictions result from landlords failing to follow the rules when renovating renters' homes:

> Despite the legal protections that are in place, there has been an increase in the number of "renovictions" throughout Canada. In practice, landlords may not provide the proper notice or the financial compensation that they are required to give renters. Furthermore, as new landlords buy up rental homes, renters who may not be aware of their legal rights, such as the right of first refusal, can find themselves pushed out of their unit, while new landlords renovate their homes and rent them out again at a higher rate.[5]

Another approach is to use "renoviction" to designate cases where tenants are evicted with N13 eviction notices. For instance, in 2019 the Advocacy Centre for Tenants Ontario documented the rise of what they call "no-fault evictions," which included evictions via N12 (for landlord's own use) and N13 notices, the latter of which they label "renoviction."[6] Media reports also sometimes identify renovictions as cases where tenants get N13s.[7]

Renovations obviously feature prominently in discussions of renoviction. Sometimes it is claimed that renoviction occurs when tenants are evicted for renovations.[8] Other times, the point of emphasis is that the renovations the landlord claims they will do are not actually done in the case of renoviction, or that the proposed renovations are not so significant that they require the tenant to vacate.[9]

These common misunderstandings of renoviction perpetuate the myth that there are landlords who follow the law to legitimately evict tenants for the purpose of upgrading rental properties, and others who abuse the system to illegitimately "renovict" tenants. More importantly, the spread of such misconceptions risks leaving tenants with the false impression that a better knowledge of the law alone will protect them against renoviction.

Renoviction, as we use the term, is when a landlord tries to push a tenant out of their home by claiming they will renovate the unit. It is a landlord strategy to permanently displace tenants from rental units based on the claim that they will renovate the empty units. The landlord begins the process of renoviction by notifying the tenant, either verbally or in writing, that they want them to move out. The landlord may then apply financial, physical, and legal pressure on the tenant to push them out of their home. The landlord may issue eviction notices, but they may not. The landlord may or may not renovate common areas of the building or individual units after tenants have moved out. Renoviction is primarily about displacement, not renovations.

While the specific provisions vary, Canadian provinces allow eviction for renovations, and landlords can renovict tenants without breaking any rules or doing anything illegal.[10] In Ontario, a landlord may legally evict a tenant to extensively renovate their rental unit.[11] The Ontario *Residential Tenancies Act* thus provides a legal framework for renoviction. When landlords do start the legal eviction process by issuing an N13 eviction notice, they frequently do not find it necessary to have evictions enforced through the legal process. This is because the combined pressure of a legal eviction notice with extralegal eviction tactics is often enough to push tenants out. When these tactics get the job done, there is no need for the landlord to file an eviction application with the Landlord and Tenant Board. Landlords do not always issue an N13 notice and initiate the legal eviction process when trying to push tenants out, but there is nothing illegal about, for example, offering tenants buyouts on the condition that they terminate their tenancies. This is not to say that landlords may not break various rules when renovicting tenants, only that it is misguided to characterize renovictions as cases where tenants are evicted "illegitimately" or "illegally." Landlords renovict and therefore permanently displace tenants even when they follow the rules or refrain from breaking any laws. We will return to this discussion at the end of this chapter.

Our understanding of renoviction is supported by the economic realities of rental housing in Toronto and across the country, how renovictions actually unfold, and public statements made by landlords. In the next chapter we examine in detail how renovictions play out. Here, we look at the other two considerations.

CLOSING RENT GAPS

A rent gap is present where there is a significant difference between actual, capitalized rent and the potential to increase the rate of rent extraction if land is given a "higher" use.[12] In cities, the presence of rent gaps, and the potential profits to be made by closing rent gaps, is a determinant of land development and rental housing production. For example, in Toronto's housing market, high-rise condo development in the core and single-family home construction in the suburbs are the dominant methods of closing rent gaps. Two recently aborted Ontario government policies would have encouraged these methods. In 2022, Ontario removed development restrictions on protected greenbelt lands, a move that would have further enabled landowners to close rent gaps through extensive suburbanization and single-family home construction had a corruption scandal not caused the government to reverse its policy.[13] That same year, Ontario passed legislation that gives the provincial government authority to limit the City of Toronto's power to regulate the demolition and conversion of rental housing buildings.[14] Although Ontario has yet to impose limits on Toronto's ability to regulate apartment building demolitions, this policy could further empower condo developers to close rent gaps through intensive development in the urban core.

Land development is not the only means by which landowners close rent gaps; landlords have also developed several techniques to close rent gaps in rental housing. When there are low rates of vacancy, tenants are forced to compete for rental units. In a competitive rental housing market, the only "higher" use landlords need to give to a rental unit to close the rent gap is a new rental contract at a higher rent price than the current tenant is paying.

In Ontario, most rental units are subject to rent control. This means that during a tenancy, the landlord can raise the rent only once per year by the provincial rent increase guideline, which is at most 2.5 percent. However, there is no limit to how much a landlord can increase the rent between tenants, so every time a rental unit is vacated the landlord can raise the rent to whatever they would like. As the asking rents for vacant units have risen significantly over the past several years, large gaps have opened up between what many sitting tenants are paying and what landlords can charge new tenants. To close such a gap, the landlord simply needs to gain vacant possession of the rental unit. Renoviction is a landlord strategy to close rent gaps in rental housing markets on a unit-by-unit basis;

to actualize the potential for increased rent extraction by evicting sitting tenants.

Rent regulations in other provinces like British Columbia and Quebec also mediate rent gaps. The rules in British Columbia are similar to Ontario's: the provincial government sets an annual rent increase guideline, but there is no limit on rent increases between tenants. When controls on rents are tied to the tenancy and not to the rental unit itself, there is what is called "vacancy decontrol." In Quebec, the regulations around how rents can be raised are attached to rental units, not tenants; landlords are not supposed to be able to get unlimited rent increases between tenants.[15] However, since 2019, average asking rents for vacant units in Montreal have increased 71 percent. Despite provincial rules that formally impose rent control on vacant units, Montreal landlords extract large rent increases from new tenants. This is because, among other reasons, tenants cannot successfully challenge these rent increases at the Quebec Rental Board without hard-to-access information that proves their rent is higher than the lowest rent paid for the unit during the twelve-month period before they moved in.[16] Renoviction thus serves the same purpose for landlords in provinces with different rent rules, permanently displacing tenants to close rent gaps on a unit-by-unit basis.

Many long-term tenants throughout Toronto are paying around $1,000 per month for a one-bedroom or two-bedroom apartment. Meanwhile, the average asking rent for a vacant one-bedroom in the city over the past few years has been around $2,300 to $2,500.[17] The removal of sitting tenants from their homes under these conditions not only allows landlords to significantly increase their rental revenues, it can also increase the value of the property as a result of these higher rents.

Landlords who use the renoviction strategy often look to urban areas where they anticipate rapid future rises in land value. They purchase older, undercapitalized, low- to medium-density rental buildings from smaller, less profitable companies. They acquire buildings with a high proportion of long-term tenants paying rents that are significantly lower than asking rents for vacant units in the area. Why would a landlord buy such a building? Because they can make a lot of money by closing the rent gaps. Additional investment in the form of extensive renovations can also result in significant returns, so long as rents are raised.

Ads and brochures for multi-family rental buildings in Toronto that are for sale often highlight rent gaps and "rental upside." Brochures will often note the "gap to market," or the average difference between rents for tenants currently in the building and market rents for the area, and how much rents can be increased if a property is "repositioned"—such properties are sometimes called "value-add." Salespeople highlight these features because they know that is what their clients are seeking. Low rents in a building are attractive not because investors like low revenues but because they mean the property's value is lower due to these rents. Long-term tenants paying lower rents are not normally looking to move—if anything because they can't afford to so landlords have to work to get tenants out and turn over units. Sometimes this is put in terms of "active management," whereby a building that is "undermanaged" is one where tenants are not being actively pushed out. Often landlords will seek to acquire these types of older buildings with lower rents even before they hit the market and are advertised to the public.

Renoviction is not the only strategy landlords use to increase rent revenues and close rent gaps. Other common landlord strategies include aggressive eviction litigation against tenants for unpaid rent or alleged behavioural infractions, eviction for landlord's own use, above guideline rent increases (AGIs), and "demovictions."[18] Some of these strategies bear some similarities to renoviction. The term is sometimes even used to describe these other landlord strategies that aim to displace sitting tenants.

An own use eviction is when a landlord evicts a tenant by claiming they, a family member, a caregiver, or someone buying the building or condo wants to move into the unit. In Ontario, landlords sometimes initiate an own use eviction by issuing an N12 eviction notice, though many own use evictions happen informally. Own use evictions are an increasingly common tactic to displace tenants in order to raise rents.[19] Landlords who pursue own use evictions are typically individuals who own multiple properties, including rental properties. Tenants who face eviction for own use often rent units in divided houses and condo buildings, although we also know of cases where tenants renting above storefronts and in purpose-built rental buildings have faced eviction for own use.[20] Sometimes landlords will conduct renovations before rerenting the apartment at a higher rate. And sometimes tenants will be told they have to move out because the landlord wants to renovate the unit before moving in themselves. Because renovations sometimes take place in the context of these evictions, and own use evictions are another way landlords seek to close rent gaps, some people will label these cases "renovictions." While we consider renovictions to be distinct from own use evictions, there is certainly some grey area, particularly since landlords sometimes emphasize their intent to renovate when informally approaching tenants to move out, and some landlords will even issue N12 notices before or after issuing N13 notices to tenants.

Provinces that limit how much landlords can raise

rents on sitting tenants each year—like British Columbia, Quebec, Ontario, Manitoba, New Brunswick, and Prince Edward Island—allow landlords to pass on certain costs to tenants through rent increases above those limits. In Ontario, landlords can apply to the LTB for an AGI to pass off costs related to eligible capital expenditures to tenants (as well as costs related to security services or an extraordinary increase in property taxes). Eligible capital expenditures include the repair or replacement of common building elements such as roofs, balconies, windows, lobbies, elevators, and heating systems. AGIs allow landlords to raise rents up to 3 percent above the provincial rent increase guideline for three successive years, placing a large financial burden on tenants and contributing to displacement.[21] Thus, AGIs and renoviction both directly contribute to the displacement of tenants, and both can involve renovations that disrupt the lives of existing tenants. However, renoviction is a more concentrated application of financial, physical, and legal displacement pressure on tenants by landlords.

Demovictions, or when tenants are evicted because the landlord intends to demolish the building, are also considered by some to be cases of renoviction. In Ontario, landlords use the same notice (i.e., an N13) to start the legal eviction process for extensive renovations and demolition of the residential complex. However, demoviction is typically initiated by landowners with development interests and capabilities. The quantity of capital that must be advanced to demolish a building and redevelop land is far greater than the capital advanced to purchase a small- or mid-sized apartment building and renovict the tenants living there. In Toronto, the municipal regulation of land uses through zoning policy requires landowners to meet specific conditions before it permits demolition and redevelopment.

Toronto imposes no such conditions on purchasers of rental housing. While demoviction and renoviction are both strategies that displace tenants to extract higher rents, renoviction allows relatively smaller quantities of capital to be valorized more quickly than demoviction. Renoviction is a strategy that is therefore more easily replicable by a larger number of smaller real estate firms. Firms that demovict tenants are typically much larger, and not only possess and have access to large amounts of capital, but also stand to profit more from redevelopment. Cities will therefore often try to obtain minor benefits or concessions from these firms in exchange for approving developments, possibly including compensation to tenants.

Once again, there can be some cases that are hard to classify. For instance, a landlord may claim on an N13 that they intend to demolish the rental unit despite only detailing extensive renovations on the notice. Or in an effort to permanently displace tenants, a small firm lacking the capital to redevelop may nevertheless tell tenants they intend to demolish a building.

Despite the similarities between renoviction, own use eviction, demoviction, and AGIs, these are distinct strategies for increasing returns. Landlords who renovict tenants cite the desire to renovate the vacant unit as the reason for forcing people out and draw from a consistent playbook of tactics well suited to displacing tenants from low- to medium-density rental properties. The number of landlords using the renoviction strategy in Toronto and other cities appeared to be growing in recent years, and many replicate it over and over in buildings they acquire. This warrants inquiry into the specific practice. And it is impossible to understand renoviction without appreciating the real estate context in which it takes place. Real estate investors are not interested in spending $10,000 or

$50,000 to upgrade a two-bedroom apartment for a tenant who is paying $1,200 a month in rent. But if the landlord can double the rent for a new tenant and sell or refinance the property following extensive renovations, then that expense becomes a worthwhile investment.

LANDLORDS SPEAK FOR THEMSELVES

Most landlords who renovict tenants try to avoid attention. They understand how the public generally feels about what they are doing, so they keep a low profile. But some landlords who use the renoviction strategy are more open about their approach to real estate investment.

Lankin Investments and Riley Real Estate Ventures (RREV) are two landlords with a track record of renoviction who market themselves to potential investors based on the profitability of the strategy.[22] Since both firms have made recent public statements about their business models, we will quote from them at length.

Lankin Investments, founded by the father and son duo Brian and Kyle Pulis and formerly known as Pulis Investments, is a rental housing investment firm involved in the "strategic acquisition and renewal of undervalued and underperforming apartment buildings."[23] In early 2022, Lankin bought the mid-rise apartment building at 1570 Lawrence Avenue West in north Toronto and issued N13 eviction notices to the building's ground-floor tenants.[24] The following month, Lankin issued an offering memo to potential investors that outlined their investment strategy and provided information about the properties owned by what the memo refers to as the "Partnership."[25]

The firm seeks to "create value" by purchasing properties they deem undervalued, conducting renovations, refinancing "to realize immediate market value gains," and using those funds to acquire new properties.[26] Of course,

Lankin Investments seeks to increase rents following renovations. This is only possible if renovated units are rented to new tenants (or, theoretically, old tenants signing new leases). In their offering memo, they note how many units in each of their properties have been renovated to date, as well as the pre-renovation rents and post-renovation rents. In many of the properties, more than half of the units have been renovated in only a few years. Often, rents in the buildings double following renovations.

The memo, as well as earlier Lankin Investments memos going back to 2016, also stated the following with respect to its properties:

> As the Partnership intends to vacate all apartment units in the Property and reposition the Property by performing significant renovations and improvements in order to lease the Property to a new demographic of tenants, the future rents, vacancy, expense, cost, and other financial information concerning the Current Properties are expected to be materially different than the historical information disclosed herein.[27]

Here, Lankin Investments articulates most clearly the strategy that is described and suggested elsewhere in the memo and the firm's promotional materials. The different tactics Lankin Investments uses to push tenants out of their homes in order to turn over units have been well documented.[28]

In a 2021 interview, Jason Thomsen of Lankin Investments elaborated on the business model:

> The revenue that we generate from these assets increases pretty significantly, and as a result, the value of the assets also increases. Once the value of the asset

> is increased substantially, what we do is we employ a program of refinancing. Refinancing basically allows us to capture equity growth that has occurred in those assets over a period of time, allows us to withdraw that equity by taking on a larger mortgage, and we use that equity to roll into new acquisitions. . . . It really creates a compounding effect for the fund, allowing us to deploy more capital year over year, allowing us to acquire more buildings which then go through the same value-add model.[29]

In the interview, Thomsen goes on to explain just how profitable the business model can be. In 2016, Lankin bought the thirty-four-unit building at 44–52 Hayden Street in Hamilton for $3.3 million.[30] In 2016, the average rent for a two-bedroom apartment in the building was $770. By 2021, two-thirds of the original tenants had been removed from the building and average rents had more than doubled, to $1,700. Thomsen notes that each "unit turn" has added $220,000 to $250,000 to the building's equity value. In 2020, the building was assessed at a total value of $9.02 million. Thomsen underlines Lankin Investments' unit-by-unit approach to closing rent gaps: "It is a significant value-add model which generates pretty strong results in a relatively short period of time . . . there are still about ten units left to go, so there's additional upside to be had."

RREV, founded by Brendan Riley, is a smaller outfit that got its start in the single-family house-flipping business before expanding into the acquisition of purpose-built rental properties. In 2021, RREV bought the twelve-unit low-rise building at 2419 Keele Street in north Toronto and issued N13 eviction notices to all tenants living there.[31] Tenants of 2419 Keele responded with a successful campaign that stopped the evictions.[32]

On its website, RREV spelled out its business model to investors:

> Working closely with our extensive industry network, our mission is to acquire undervalued properties, efficiently execute on extensive renovations, stabilize the building at today's market rent rates resulting in us refinancing or selling the property. The proven and efficient process will ensure that we can continually guarantee the capital returns expected from our investors.[33]

Referring to the model as "proven" suggests RREV had executed it multiple times before. And thanks to media coverage, we know of one other case for sure, at 1 Kingswood Road in east Toronto. The company at one point also listed newly renovated apartments for rent at a few other low-rise apartment buildings throughout Toronto. When asked why he had issued eviction notices for extensive renovations to tenants at the Kingswood Road building, Riley explained his approach this way: "We are improving the quality of the building and therefore the quality of the tenants that will be living there in the future."[34]

As with Lankin Investments, renoviction is central to RREV's business model. Tenants are not pushed out as a by-product of renovation work. Rather, renovations are conducted so that rents can be raised to market rates, which is only possible if tenants are permanently displaced. This is done to provide returns for investors. In one Facebook post, RREV claims to "help create environments of opportunity . . . by unlocking the value of underperforming properties across the GTA. We have helped countless partners build passive income and reach financial freedom through safe, secure investments in #realestate."[35]

Another post explains how RREV "unlocks" this value through the "#BRRRRMethod: Buy, Rehab, Rent, Refinance, Repeat." In a video posted to the RREV YouTube channel, Shane Newman, director of finance, shared this candid reflection on why investors are attracted to RREV's business model:

> They see us as opportunistic. It has somewhat of a negative connotation sometimes, but in this situation we are opportunistic. We're looking at opportunity in the marketplace that pretty much no one else has jumped on. And we're extracting the maximum amount of value we can on that opportunity.[36]

Though RREV is one of the few firms publicly advertising how they want to exploit such "opportunity in the marketplace," Newman was wrong to think that they were virtually alone in executing the strategy. This is made clear by the number of buildings in Toronto and elsewhere where tenants face renoviction and the similarities in how these renovictions are carried out, as well as the number of individuals and firms who have used the strategy across different buildings.

Some landlords will advertise their renoviction strategy indirectly by partnering with a third party that brings in other investors. For example, Addy is a real estate investment platform that allows members to invest as little as one dollar in properties and says its mission is "to enable every human to own real estate."[37] When Addy launches a new property on its website for members to buy shares of, it provides an offering memo outlining the landlord's strategy for the property. Not long before tenants began experiencing renoviction at two north Toronto properties that were listed on Addy's website, the offering memos for the properties made clear that Addy members were being invited to invest in and profit from renoviction.

The memos outline how the landlords intend to generate a profit by renovating the properties over a five-year period and then selling. One property is made up of ninety-five units spread across nineteen low-rise buildings; the other is ninety-nine units in nine low-rise buildings. In one case, the landlord "plans to renovate the buildings and increase the below market rents (currently 1-bedroom at $1,056/month and 2-bedroom at $1,135/ month) to market (currently 1-bedroom at $1,750/month and 2-bedroom at $2,150/month)."[38] In the other case, the landlord "plans to renovate the buildings and increase below market rents (currently 1-bed at $1,027/month and 2-bed at $1,519/ month) to market (1-bed at $1,800/month and 2-bed units at $2,900/month, at year 1)."[39] Over the course of five years the landlords intend to permanently displace all of the existing tenants, at a rate of around twenty per year. Prospective investors are told that this is going to be achieved through the use of "financial incentives," or buy-outs. Although both memos outline extensive renovation programs for each unit, it is made clear that renovations will only be conducted in units that tenants are pushed out of and that the projected increases in rent are dependent on tenants being forced out. The memos also shed some light on how lucrative the landlords expect renoviction to be: in one case a profit of over $18 million is anticipated on an investment of $46 million, in the other a profit of over $30 million is promised on an investment of $61 million.

Landlords renovict tenants to close rent gaps and increase the value of their properties. Many will then leverage this value to acquire more rental properties, where they can deploy the strategy again. Vacancy decontrol and rent regulations across provinces establish the legal framework through which the closing of rent gaps is profitable on a per unit basis. Landlords attract further capital investment by demonstrating to potential investors that their renoviction strategy is quick and cost-effective and may be carried out across multiple properties simultaneously. In this way, over time, landlords may increase the scale at which they deploy the renoviction strategy.

THE LEGAL PROCESS OF EVICTION AND THE RIGHT TO RETURN

Canadian provincial and territorial landlord-tenant laws allow landlords to evict tenants for renovations.[40] Ontario landlord-tenant law explicitly and purposefully allows for landlords to evict tenants for extensive renovations.[41] And while landlords may be required to show they have obtained or applied for permits from the appropriate authorities to carry out renovation work, the law does not require that work to be in any way necessary. Landlords in Ontario can seek to evict tenants at the LTB in order to extensively renovate and remodel apartments that are in perfectly acceptable condition and when tenants have no major issues with the state of repair of their units.

During the parliamentary debate on the Ontario *Residential Tenancies Act*, a Liberal member of provincial parliament (MPP) opined on the role of renovations in raising rental buildings and districts to "higher" uses: "I think this bill will create . . . the ability for many investors to keep investing to renovate many falling down buildings, many areas to be cleaned, to be up to code, to be fit in the neighbourhood."[42]

With renoviction, buildings and districts are "cleaned," not by upgrading the built environment, but through the removal of working-class tenants whose long-term tenancies have contributed to the depression of local rents and property values. The *Residential Tenancies Act* establishes the legal framework through which this process is mediated and may be enforced.

The legal process of eviction for extensive renovations is straightforward, inexpensive, and accessible to landlords. The process comprises multiple stages in which landlords and the state apply escalating levels of legal, financial, and physical pressure on tenants to move out. Landlords' financial resources typically allow them to employ property managers, real estate agents, contractors, engineers, paralegals, and lawyers at each stage of the process to advance their case and secure their desired outcome. In the end, the legal process is set up to sanction and enforce evictions. Individual working-class tenants have no comparable legal or organizational support to rely on. Having slight financial resources despite working long hours makes it very difficult for individual working-class tenants to respond to, and navigate through, the legal process imposed on them. Tenants are thus confronted by a legal process that is designed to dispossess them of their homes.

Each stage in the legal eviction process for extensive renovations is initiated by either the landlord or the LTB. The landlord starts the legal process when they issue an N13 eviction notice to the tenant. In the N13, the landlord details the work they plan to do in the unit and indicates a termination date that must be at least 120 days from the date the notice is issued. The tenant is not obligated to move out by the termination date in the notice. The termination date is only the soonest possible date that the tenant could be legally ordered to vacate the unit by the LTB.

To get an actual eviction order on the basis of an N13, the landlord has to file an eviction application with the LTB, which the landlord can do at any time from the day after they issue the N13 to the tenant up to thirty days after the termination date stated in the N13. When the landlord files the eviction application, they may include with the application additional information to support their case, such as reports from engineers or contractors and permits from municipal or regulatory authorities. Once the LTB receives the landlord's eviction application, it processes the application, assigns it a file number, and schedules a hearing where an adjudicator will hear the case.

Tenants who receive a notice of hearing from the LTB face the potential of imminent eviction by order of the board. In advance of their eviction hearing, tenants must either try to secure legal representation or prepare to self-represent and present a case in opposition to their landlord's eviction application. Ahead of the hearing, tenants may need to consider making decisions about the loss of wages from taking time off work, child care arrangements, language interpretation, and technology and internet access, just to attend and participate in the online hearing. As a result, many tenants do not attend their eviction hearings.

In cases where the LTB decides to terminate the tenancy, the board's order indicates the date by which the tenant must vacate the unit. The soonest the LTB may order the tenancy terminated is eleven days from the date of its order, although in consideration of the tenant's circumstances, it may give the tenant more time to vacate. When the LTB orders eviction, the tenant must vacate their home by the termination date in the LTB order or else face potential removal by the sheriff.

Landlords can file LTB eviction orders with the sheriff's office to have evictions enforced. After the landlord files an eviction order with the sheriff, the sheriff's office notifies the tenant of the date of the scheduled eviction enforcement. The sheriff coordinates the enforcement of the eviction with the landlord and attends the tenant's unit to oversee the changing of the locks. If the tenant is present in the unit at the time of enforcement, the sheriff will remove the tenant from the unit, possibly with the help of police.

While the specific procedures vary between provinces, eviction enforcement is similar across Canada. Landlords file with the designated provincial authority to get an eviction order. In some cases, there is a hearing in front of an adjudicator who decides the case; in other cases, an officer reviews a paper application and decides on whether to issue an eviction order. If the tenant does not move out by the termination date in the order, the landlord can request that the order be enforced by provincial court officers such as sheriffs or bailiffs.

Ontario's *Residential Tenancies Act* says that a tenant who receives an eviction notice for extensive renovations may return to live in the rental unit at their previous rent once the landlord completes renovations.[43] In reality, this is simply not something that happens. Tenants who are evicted for extensive renovations do not exercise this "right of first refusal" and move back into their homes after the work is completed.

In practice, a renovicted tenant has no legal recourse to regain occupancy of an apartment once the landlord has rerented the unit to another tenant. This legal precedent was established in the case of 795 College Street in Toronto. The landlords, Evan Johnsen and Neil Spiegel, renovicted tenants from the building and prevented them from returning to their homes by rerenting them to new tenants paying higher rents. Some of the tenants took their case to the LTB, only for the board to rule that "the Legislature did not intend reinstatement of the tenancy to be an available remedy" to tenants.[44]

Even if a landlord does not prevent tenants from returning to their homes by surreptitiously bringing in new tenants at higher rents, consider what would be required of a tenant to actually exercise the right to return. N13 notices often say the renovations will take anywhere from seven to twelve months or more. A tenant therefore has to find long-term accommodations, which for most working-class tenants means entering into a new one-year lease agreement. The same math that makes it profitable for a landlord to renovict tenants means that a tenant will typically be unable to find an apartment nearby that they can afford. Moving costs and the increased rent the tenant has to pay will affect them. The tenant's work and personal life may also be disrupted by the move. If the renovations are completed in several months, it can be difficult for the tenant to get out of their lease and financially unviable to carry two leases. Bear in mind, though, that the law does not hold the landlord to any timeline for the completion of renovations. The longer the landlord drags things out, the more likely it is that the tenant will decide to move on for good. As time passes, the changes to the tenant's life become solidified in their new home, making it more difficult to simply cut ties again and move back to the previous home.

Much of the discourse surrounding renoviction uncritically fixates on legal issues. According to the City of Toronto, renoviction only occurs when the landlord either does not carry out extensive renovations or does not allow the evicted tenant to return to the unit.

The first version of the City's eviction prevention handbook, created as a result of the City taking an interest in renoviction, contains a "checklist for illegitimate eviction notice."[45] The checklist contains criteria by which tenants are meant to assess whether or not they have received a valid eviction notice. One of the criteria listed is that the eviction notice must "have a legitimate reason and one made in good faith." Yet as we saw above, regardless of what their landlord plans to do, a tenant who receives an N13 notice has received a legal eviction notice for a legitimate reason: extensive renovations. A tenant on the receiving end of such a notice may have no reason to doubt that the landlord intends to renovate the unit. The more important questions are: What is the landlord's primary motivation for issuing the notice? And what will happen to the tenant if they move out? Renoviction is, first and foremost, about displacement, not renovations. And we know that if the tenant moves out, they are exceedingly unlikely to ever return to their home. Narrowly focusing on whether landlords are following certain rules to evict tenants for renovations is inappropriate when their objective is displacement. Even when a landlord actually intends to conduct extensive renovations, tenants do not need to submit to eviction.

By focusing on the narrow legal question of whether the eviction notice is "illegitimate," the City of Toronto's handbook serves only to facilitate displacement. The handbook even encourages tenants to try to assert their right of first refusal, without mentioning that landlords prevent tenants from returning to their units or that the legal precedent set by 795 College Street sanctions this. The handbook advises tenants who have received N13 notices: "If you would like to move back into your units after renovations, be sure to indicate to your landlord—in writing—and follow through based on the timeline of the repairs."[46] Again, the City is advising tenants on the baseless assumption that landlords will allow them to move back at some point after they vacate the unit.

Landlords do not need to flout eviction rules to

renovict tenants. They rely on a set of legal and extralegal tactics to push tenants out of their homes. In cases where the landlord issues N13 eviction notices and files eviction applications against tenants at the LTB, the landlord does so in compliance with the law, not in contravention to it. Landlords engage with the legal eviction process because it is more likely to serve their objective of displacing tenants than it is to protect tenants from eviction.

It should be clear by now that the success of the landlord's renoviction strategy does not hinge on the tenant being unaware of the right of first refusal. Once the tenant has vacated, the landlord can easily prevent them from ever returning to the unit. Fines are not a deterrent to landlords here, as such costs are easily recouped through the increased rents they can collect from new tenants and the increase in the value of the property resulting from renoviction.

By focusing narrowly on legal issues and conflating renoviction with the physical rehabilitation of rental housing, cities like Toronto and non-profit organizations suggest that they are not opposed to renoviction, so long as it is by the book. Either that, or they are under the mistaken impression that if no laws are violated, tenants will not be displaced.

If it were actually the case that the apparent rise of renovictions in Toronto was a result of a frantic, city-wide blitz by landlords to install condo-style elements in low-rent buildings, we would still be obliged to challenge the City's and non-profits' prioritization of kitchen islands over the preservation of the tenancies of working-class renters. But such a view is only possible if one fundamentally misunderstands why landlords renovict tenants and how renovictions actually play out. Once more: the objective of landlords who renovict tenants is to permanently displace them from their homes and raise rents on vacant units.

TWO

The Landlord Playbook

Landlords initiate renovictions in different ways. For instance, they may send a text message telling tenants they have to move out, or go door to door offering tenants buy-outs, or just slip N13 eviction notices under everyone's doors. How things then unfold will depend on the landlord's approach and commitment to forcing tenants out, how tenants respond, and how these factors influence each other. But despite the variety of tactics landlords may use and the different ways things may play out, there are significant similarities across cases and a number of steps that we can think of as the landlord playbook. This chapter examines how renovictions play out by analyzing the different actions landlords take to displace tenants. Landlords do not always take the same steps, nor in the same sequence, but the moves in the playbook are commonly used, often in the sequence described below, and represent escalations in pressure to push tenants out of their homes.

As we have noted, we are most familiar with how renovictions play out in buildings in Toronto, and this chapter is based on our familiarity with around two hundred buildings in the city where renoviction took place and extensive interviews with over two dozen Toronto tenants. However, we also conducted interviews with tenants and organizers in Hamilton, Ottawa, Halifax, and Montreal to supplement publicly available information about renoviction in other cities across the country, which generally unfolds along similar lines.

THE SALE

Tenants identify the sale of their buildings as a point in time when they face acute displacement pressures. Occasionally landlords will initiate a renoviction before selling a building in order to make the property more attractive to buyers, who can charge high rents for those vacant units. Realtors and other agents may help push tenants out in preparation for a sale. Often, though, a new landlord will acquire a building, then try to push the existing tenants out so they can raise rents.

Over the past several years, renovictions have been common in Toronto when low-rise apartment buildings or apartments above storefronts on main streets change hands. These are buildings of two to four storeys, typically with four to twenty apartments, though sometimes more. If existing tenants are paying rents that are considered below market, then landlords acquiring these buildings can generate significant returns by evicting those tenants and bringing in new tenants at much higher rents. As mentioned earlier, when these types of buildings are for sale, ads will frequently mention "rental upside" or highlight the gap between the rents paid by existing tenants and rents for vacant units in the area. If renovations are completed and new tenants are brought in at higher rents, a building can either be sold again for a profit or held as an income-generating asset.

Tenants living in rooming houses and single-family homes divided into multiple units also face renoviction. However, landlords often try to push tenants out of such buildings at the time of a sale by claiming they, a family member, or the new buyer intends to move in (i.e., an own use eviction). Meanwhile, tenants living in larger purpose-built rental buildings often face displacement pressures when their buildings are sold thanks to disruptive renovations to common areas, balconies, and other parts of a building that can be used as the basis for an above guideline increase in rent. Larger firms and those with institutional backing seem to favour a repositioning strategy centred around AGIs. Tenants in larger buildings sometimes face renoviction, but it does not appear to be the tactic of choice for the landlords possessing the capital needed to acquire these buildings. One exception is Lankin Investments, a firm that has grown considerably in recent years by renovicting tenants to "add value" to rental assets, which it then uses to expand its portfolio and attract additional investors.[1]

Landlords who acquire buildings and try to renovict tenants are typically either individual owners, partnerships, or small real estate firms using funds raised from investors. Many of these individuals, partnerships, and firms engage in the practice repeatedly, sometimes acquiring larger buildings over time as they increase their capital. In order to hide their identities, landlords acquire buildings via numbered companies or corporations simply bearing the name of the building address. Occasionally these firms may have a public profile, but even in these cases the landlords will try to hide their identities from the tenants they are trying to renovict. For example, Brendan Riley ran RREV, which had a website that advertised its practices to prospective investors. However, when Riley acquired a building he did so through a company with a generic name created just for that purpose, and when presenting himself to tenants he would claim to merely be an agent of the landlord. Similarly, Lankin Investments is a real estate investment firm that advertises its business strategy to prospective investors through its website, offering memos, and promotional materials. Lankin also has a property management arm, Drake Property Management, with a much smaller public profile. When Lankin acquires a building, tenants are introduced to Drake Property Management, thus hiding Lankin's involvement. Hiding their true identity not only shields a landlord from potential backlash as they seek to renovict tenants, it also adds to the uncertainty, confusion, and stress for many tenants facing renoviction.

INITIAL APPROACHES

Landlords often initiate renovictions by approaching tenants informally after acquiring a building. The landlord or an agent will explain that the building has been acquired and there are plans to conduct renovations. At this early stage, tenants may simply be encouraged to move out because of the extensive and disruptive renovations. Sometimes this is presented as being in the tenants' own interests, as the planned renovations will allegedly soon make it very uncomfortable to live in the building. But tenants are often simply told that everyone in the building will have to move out because of the renovations. The new landlord has a plan for the building and it does not include the existing tenants. For example, one tenant recalled that the first time they met their new landlord they were told, "We have plans for your building. You guys have to leave because we're going to renovate your unit." Another tenant was told by their new landlord, "We bought the building. Now we are going to renovate. We need every tenant to move out." In another instance, a tenant was told by a landlord representative that the new owners planned to add a storey to the building and, as a result, the tenant would have to vacate.

Notably, tenants will be approached individually by

the landlord or their agent. Typically this will happen in person at the building, with the landlord or agent going door to door, though sometimes letters will be sent to tenants instead. Tenants may be given notices or letters explaining that the new landlord plans to renovate or may simply be told of the plans. Given the power imbalance between a landlord and a single tenant, such one-on-one interactions are to the landlord's advantage. Tenants may even be discouraged from speaking with their neighbours about the issue because "everyone's situation is different" or for "privacy reasons." If a landlord acquires multiple adjacent buildings, they may approach tenants in one building at a time, thus decreasing the number of tenants who can alert neighbours about the landlord's plans.

Despite the landlord or agent introducing themselves to tenants, they typically provide very little information about themselves. Landlords renovicting tenants hide behind property managers, realtors, and paralegals, and will often provide only phone numbers or email addresses, often generic ones (for example, tenants.416@gmail.com). In one case, a landlord presented a business card that had only their first name and a phone number. While handing out business cards is uncommon, taking steps to hide one's identity from tenants is standard. Since many buildings are acquired from long-time owners who tenants may have had a personal relationship with, such informality may not initially seem out of place. However, once they have been told that they have to leave their homes, the lack of information tenants have about the landlord can be disorienting.

It is common for landlords to offer buyouts at this stage to encourage tenants to leave. Such offers may be merely verbal or be made in writing, and they may come via intermediaries like a paralegal. For example, tenants at one low-rise building in north Toronto were approached individually by a real estate agent working with the new landlord and offered buyouts as part of what they called a "voluntary move out," rather than facing eviction through the Landlord and Tenant Board. A few thousand dollars, or even ten thousand dollars, may be offered initially if tenants agree to end their tenancy. In order to pressure tenants into taking the buyout, such offers may be presented as being available for only a limited time or being the best offer tenants will see.

Some landlords offer to cover moving expenses and may even offer to help tenants find a new place. Tenants at one building in Parkdale were contacted repeatedly by a company that allegedly facilitated building transitions and offered tenants money to attend meetings, in an effort to get them to move out.

Many tenants do move out at this stage, for a variety of reasons. First, a tenant may be planning to move out already when the landlord comes by and offers them a buyout. Second, tenants who have moved into the building more recently may already be paying higher rents than many of their neighbours and may not have strong ties to the neighbourhood; thus, a buyout may appear attractive to them and rents elsewhere may not be unobtainable. Third, a tenant may be unfamiliar with the current rental market and not realize that the difference in rent they will subsequently have to pay will quickly deplete the buyout. Tenants who have spent decades in the same apartment and do not have home internet may be particularly prone to such miscalculation. Fourth, a tenant may move out because they do not think they are allowed to refuse the offer from the landlord. If someone believes that a landlord in Ontario has the right to simply kick people out of their homes, they will think they have no choice here. Fifth, a tenant may move out because they fear a formal eviction notice is coming and either do not think this process can be successfully challenged or do not want to face that stressful situation. Sometimes landlords or their agents will say explicitly that N13 eviction notices will follow if tenants do not "voluntarily" accept a buyout, or they may just hint at this. On other occasions, tenants may simply suspect that N13 notices will follow the buyouts. One tenant who refused several buyout offers from their new landlord noted, "Most of the people who moved out . . . said they had to move out, if not there would be court proceedings."

Landlords often tell tenants that accepting a buyout now is a better alternative than being evicted by the LTB later. Faced with the potential threat of forced removal from their homes, many tenants do accept small sums of money in exchange for ending their tenancies and moving out. Landlords know that lower-income tenants are particularly susceptible to buyout pressure because they are more likely to have urgent, immediate expenses and debts. By applying buyout pressure on tenants, landlords use the social power of money to discipline and displace uncooperative, low-income tenants.[2]

Moving out after being approached informally or being offered a buyout does not, therefore, mean freely agreeing to leave one's home. Many tenants who leave their homes at this stage do not want to (the fourth and fifth cases above). And taking a buyout with the threat of eviction hanging over one's head is far from a voluntary decision. Speaking to their neighbours can help tenants resist these initial approaches and buyout offers. Not only may tenants learn that they can indeed refuse the offer, but they may be more confident in doing so knowing that they are not confronting the situation alone.

However, simply informing tenants of their rights is not enough to stop people from moving out at this stage.

If tenants do not believe they can successfully fight back in the event they are issued N13 notices, or have not heard of cases of tenants successfully beating renoviction, refusing buyout offers may not seem like a genuine option. Even if tenants know that they cannot afford asking rents in their neighbourhood or elsewhere in the city, they may leave their homes due to the stress caused by no longer feeling secure there.

The way these initial approaches by landlords take place leaves little doubt about the motives behind them. These approaches do not result from a genuine desire to improve the living conditions of existing tenants or from some recognition that the building just acquired is old and in need of work. Landlords do not propose to fix things that tenants want fixed inside their units or to address pressing issues, but focus on things like completely gutting, redesigning, and renovating the inside of units or doing extensive electrical and plumbing work within units. Tenants are not consulted about the work being proposed for their homes. There are no efforts made to conduct work in a manner that would allow tenants to remain in their homes, no meetings held with tenants about such possibilities. If the goal was to improve conditions for existing tenants, then at the very least we would expect discussions to be held with tenants about issues that exist in their units and what, if any, upgrades they thought were needed. But this is not what happens. Instead, tenants are told that they have to leave or should leave because the landlord has plans for the building that clearly do not include them. How landlords conduct themselves makes it plain that they are not primarily concerned with renovating units but with pushing existing tenants out.

Even though buildings where renovictions happen may be several decades old, they are typically not rundown or in any worse shape than neighbouring buildings. Insofar as they may need some repairs, that is not the work that is proposed in order to push tenants out. That the buildings may be older and have not been extensively renovated means that rents will typically be low—and that is the salient factor.

It is impossible to say just how common renoviction is or how many tenants move out at this early stage because there is no reliable tracking of such informal approaches from landlords. Though tenants have reported many cases of renoviction that were initiated informally, we do not know what share of cases are reported. It is less likely that a case will be reported if there are few units in a building and tenants move out after being approached informally. Furthermore, tenants living in houses divided into only a few units or shared with the landlord may be more inclined to move out after being approached informally because they do not know they can fight the renoviction or do not want the stress of living in a house with someone who wants them out and who can make life difficult by escalating in the ways described below. In our experience, a renoviction that is initiated outside the period of a sale is more likely to be at a home divided into a few rental units, rather than a low-rise building or apartments above storefronts, however, renovictions are sometimes initiated by long-time landlords at these other types of properties when no sale is imminent.

NEGLECT

A landlord is responsible for maintaining the property. It is undeniable that landlords frequently fail to adequately maintain properties, neglecting both common areas and issues inside of units. Such failure is the norm, and often particularly acute, in the case of renoviction. After all, landlords renovicting tenants have no interest in being a landlord to the existing tenants who are paying reasonable rents. Neglecting the property not only saves them money, but it also increases the pressure on tenants to leave.

Tenants often notice a change in standards once their building is sold. Basic maintenance like cutting the grass, snow removal, and the cleaning of common areas will become less frequent or cease entirely. Garbage removal may also be interrupted or inconsistent. One tenant told us: "The previous landlord would clean the common spaces every week. The common spaces were now going several weeks without anybody coming by to clean. . . . They wouldn't take out the garbage. I was emailing them every week for four weeks telling them the garbage wasn't taken out." Another tenant reported that after the garbage started piling up at the building due to the new landlord's neglect, the landlord offered them fifty dollars a month to take out the garbage.

On-site superintendents are often let go, which cuts costs and vacates a unit. They are "replaced" by property managers or other agents working remotely. This means that routine cleaning and maintenance of common areas will not get done, or not as frequently or as well, and that issues like burned-out lightbulbs in common areas or broken intercom systems will go unnoticed by management. It also means there is no one at the building with a master key in case a tenant loses their key or in the event of a medical emergency inside a unit. One tenant recalled how, when a neighbour lost their keys: "No one picked up the emergency line, and no one was coming. We were looking at either him spending the weekend in a homeless shelter or all the tenants getting together and calling a locksmith and just paying for it, to get him back in his house."

When a tenant tries to contact the new landlord about

such issues, they are often frustrated. In most cases, tenants are provided with a phone number or email address to contact for maintenance or in case of emergency. It is common for calls to simply go to voicemail and not be returned, and for emails to not be responded to. One tenant noted, "It wasn't just that they were neglecting maintenance. It's that it became impossible to actually request maintenance."

Requests for in-unit repairs are often ignored in the early stages of renoviction. Tenants report having to call or email their landlords repeatedly to request maintenance. When requests are actually acknowledged, the work itself is often not done or is done only poorly after some delay. One tenant reported, "We did send them, at least three times, a list of all the things that were wrong in all the apartments and in the building. It took them a year, and still they did not get through that list." Another tenant noted how even when they would speak to the new property manager directly about their maintenance issues, their requests for repairs in their bathroom would be ignored: "He'd tell me to put it in writing. And every time I put it in writing he didn't do anything about it." Tenants facing renoviction often decide to simply stop requesting maintenance because doing so seems pointless. One tenant sent repeated requests to management over the course of several months to repair a leak in their ceiling. Rather than address the issue, management encouraged the tenant to accept the buyout that had been offered. Some tenants also fear that alerting the landlord to disrepair will just provide the landlord with an excuse to kick them out.

In many cases, there is no office address tenants can go to in an effort to press their maintenance concerns. If tenants are even given an address for the landlord, it may simply be a PO box number. For example, the address of Evan Johnsen and Neil Spiegel's property management company,

Anchor, is a mailbox. Even Lankin Investments, which has an office, lists only a PO box as the address of their property management arm, Drake Property Management. In another case, the landlord's listed address was a mailbox at a United Parcel Service store.

Unfortunately, none of this is surprising. Renoviction is not about a landlord conducting renovations or upgrading apartments for the benefit of existing tenants. Landlords renovicting tenants want existing tenants to move out and to do so on their timeline. Maintaining the property and conducting in-unit repairs makes tenants more comfortable in their homes and makes it easier for them to resist pressure to move out—this is antithetical to the landlord's main objective. Neglecting the property makes tenants feel unwelcome, creates additional stress, frustration, and discomfort, and can also introduce security concerns (e.g., when front doors are left open by construction workers or locks break). While these issues often arise immediately after a new landlord takes over, they can intensify as time goes on, as we will discuss below.

Neighbours coming together as a group may not only help them cope with the psychological impacts of the landlord's neglect, but can often lead to improved maintenance at a building. Tenants facing renoviction typically have more success getting maintenance issues looked after when they approach the landlord collectively about such issues. When tenants at three Toronto buildings owned by the same firm were unable to get their landlord to respond to their maintenance concerns, they set up a meeting with a property manager to view a newly renovated apartment at another of the company's properties. Upon meeting the manager for the viewing, tenants presented their collective maintenance demands.

Another avenue available to tenants when a landlord

is failing to maintain a building is to contact the municipal government and make a complaint under property standards bylaws. For example, the City of Toronto's RentSafeTO, a bylaw enforcement program for buildings of three or more storeys and ten or more units, functions as an intermediary between tenants and landlords. If a tenant submits a maintenance request to their landlord and sees no action, they can contact RentSafeTO to submit a complaint. If a bylaw enforcement officer determines that there is a violation of building standards, they will contact the landlord and request the issue be resolved.

Tenants who reach out to the City in the hopes of getting their landlord to fulfill their basic responsibilities report mixed experiences. While a call from a City building inspector may in some cases pressure landlords who neglect to maintain their properties, tenants frequently report their RentSafeTO file being closed by the City once the building inspector makes contact with the landlord, whether or not any action is taken to address their issue. In cases where the City does attempt to enforce its bylaws, landlords frequently do not comply and drag out the case for months or years by appealing the City's order. In that RentSafeTO encourages tenants to depend on a third-party intermediary that is often incapable of effectively enforcing City bylaws against landlords, it may only further frustrate and disorient tenants who face renoviction.

N13 AND OTHER EVICTION NOTICES

Issuing N13 eviction notices significantly increases the pressure on tenants to leave their homes. While tenants can ignore informal approaches and buyouts, a formal eviction notice is the first step in the legal eviction process that can result in a tenant being ordered evicted by an adjudicator at the LTB and removed from their home by a sheriff. An N13 is a notice to end a tenancy "because the landlord wants to demolish the rental unit, repair it or convert it to another use." A landlord checking off Reason 2 on the notice is claiming: "I require the rental unit to be vacant in order to do repairs or renovations so extensive that I am required to get a building permit and the rental unit must be vacant to do the work."[3] On the first page of an N13 notice, a landlord notes the date by which they want the tenant to move out—which is called "the termination date"—and details about the work they are claiming they will do.

Sometimes landlords issue N13 notices almost immediately after acquiring a building. For example, Brendan Riley issued N13 notices to all twelve tenants at 2419 Keele Street just days after acquiring the property. Often, though, if N13 notices are issued they will follow informal attempts to push tenants out or come at least a few months after a building is sold. Regardless of when the notices come, they are almost always simply slipped under apartment doors, allowing landlords to avoid facing the people they are evicting.

Michael Klein—who has renovicted tenants at buildings he owns across Ontario—developed a sophisticated approach to issuing N13 notices in some of his buildings. While Klein issued N13 notices to all tenants in buildings he had recently acquired, he also issued N13s in waves in buildings he had owned for some time.[4] For example, N13s would be given to several long-term tenants, then a few months later N13s would be issued to a different group of long-term tenants. Though Klein runs Family Properties and the buildings where tenants face renoviction are listed on the company's website, each building is typically owned by a different company generically named after the building's address or street.[5] Klein's N13 notices typically come with a cover letter offering tenants a buyout if they give up their tenancies prior to the termination date on the N13. Tenants receiving N13s from Klein have also been offered renovated apartments in the same building at significantly higher rents than they are currently paying. Tenants in these buildings also report having had great difficulty getting in-unit repairs done over the years. However, when tenants move out after receiving N13 notices from Klein, their apartments will be extensively renovated.

The whole process of renoviction can be incredibly stressful for tenants and disrupt their lives in profound ways. This is particularly true after tenants receive N13 notices. One tenant who received an N13 notice soon after their building was sold said:

> When our new landlord gave us the N13 notice it didn't feel like home anymore. And it sucks because I work from home. Having that peace of mind at home—he kind of took away, when he did what he did. . . . We were very stressed. It wasn't very peaceful. Our home didn't feel like home anymore. . . . It could be taken away from us at any time.

Another tenant we spoke with expressed similar sentiments, saying, "It was a lot of stress. . . . I also lost the feeling of privacy in my apartment. . . . I felt like someone was breathing down my neck and didn't want me there. So I no longer felt safe." Another tenant said, about receiving their N13 notice, "It was nerve-racking." "It's always in the back of your mind," their neighbour added. Tenants may even start to pack in preparation for a potential move or start to get rid of things because they anticipate having to downsize if they leave their home, which can create additional anxiety.

Some tenants take the N13 notice to be equivalent to

an eviction order and so move out, not realizing that the notice is only the first step in the legal eviction process. An N13 looks like an official document and within a thick black bar in the middle it says, "This is a legal notice that could lead to you being evicted from your home." If eviction is understood as being removed by a sheriff or other authority, then it is no surprise tenants may want to move out before that happens. Below the black bar, bolded text continues, "I am giving you this notice because I want to end your tenancy. I want you to move out of your rental unit by the following termination date: [date]." If tenants are not familiar with the legal eviction process, their landlord telling them they want them to leave can be enough for them to do so. It can also be difficult for tenants to understand precisely what the notice says if their first language is not English or because of stress.

But many tenants move out after receiving N13 notices even though they understand they do not have to. As with tenants accepting buyouts, tenants may move out at this stage for a variety of reasons. First, a tenant may be planning to move out already or may have recently moved into the building. In these cases, tenants are unlikely to challenge eviction. Second, a tenant may move out because they believe they will be able to move back into their unit at their current rent once the renovations are completed. Tenants may come to believe this because of information contained in the N13 notice or because they receive some unfortunate advice. Third, a tenant may move out because they do not think they can fight the eviction, possibly because they believe the landlord will conduct the work claimed in the notice. Fourth, a tenant may move out because they may not think fighting the eviction will be successful or because such a fight appears too stressful to manage. We will discuss the second, third, and fourth cases in turn.

On the first page of an N13 notice there is the following sentence: "You have the right to move back into the rental unit once I have completed the repairs or renovations." This line pertains to cases where the landlord seeks to end a tenancy due to extensive renovations, and after the line are instructions for a tenant should they want to move back post-renovations. As discussed earlier, tenants returning to their units post-renovations after receiving N13 notices is not something that happens. This is completely unsurprising once renoviction is understood as being a way for landlords to permanently displace tenants. On a few occasions, we have come across tenants who believed they would be able to return to their homes post-renovations because it said so on their N13. It seems likely that some tenants move out for this reason. However, in our experience, most tenants who are familiar with the supposed right to return hear about it from a non-profit, a legal professional, or a politician or politician's office. As we discussed in chapter 1, many such individuals and organizations wrongly believe that the reason tenants face "illegitimate" eviction is because they are unaware of their rights, including their right of first refusal. As a result, they assure tenants they have this right and encourage tenants who receive N13 notices to simply "assert" it. By doing so, these individuals and organizations only facilitate displacement; they have given tenants the false impression that once the renovations are completed in their units they will be able to return.[6]

Another reason a tenant may move out after receiving an N13, even if they understand it is not an eviction order, is because they think they cannot fight the eviction. The situation may appear straightforward to them: their landlord wants to do extensive renovations and is telling them they have to move out; they have no reason to doubt the landlord wants to do those renovations; so they have to move out. The second page of an N13 notice says a tenant does not have to move out if they "disagree with what the landlord has put in this notice." Tenants may not be in a position to disagree that the landlord intends to conduct such renovations or that the renovations require vacant possession—they may lack this knowledge or insight. If tenants take these to be the only grounds on which they may challenge their eviction, they may choose not to wait for a potential hearing. It is hard to say how many tenants move out for this reason. Since such tenants are unlikely to organize with their neighbours or try to fight the renoviction, they may just quietly move out.

A tenant may also move out after receiving an N13 notice because they have not heard of tenants successfully fighting back against renoviction. News stories about tenants facing renoviction, or about the rise in renovictions, are relatively common. Less common are news stories about tenants successfully fighting to keep their homes, although there have been at least several such cases. Once again this illustrates how simply informing tenants of their rights is not the best way to support tenants fighting renoviction. Telling tenants they can stay in their home and try to challenge their eviction at the board is not as enticing as some may think. For tenants, that means living with disrepair, stress, and uncertainty, and often escalating harassment and disruptions to one's daily life while waiting for an adjudicator to decide if the renovations the landlord claims they want to do are so extensive as to require vacant possession. As we discuss in the next chapter, even when talking with neighbours and getting organized does not lead to a proactive campaign against the landlord to withdraw the N13 notices, it can help tenants withstand pressure from the landlord and stay in their homes.

Landlords will also sometimes issue other formal eviction notices when trying to renovict tenants. After acquiring a building, the new landlord may begin aggressively issuing eviction notices to end a tenancy for non-payment of rent as a way to harass tenants or in the hopes that some will simply move out when they receive the notice. Sometimes this is in the context of trying to pressure tenants into transitioning from paying rent by cheque to signing up for automatic withdrawal rent payments. For example, in one case where tenants refused to sign up for automatic withdrawal payments, they received eviction notices for non-payment even though they had paid rent on time because, the landlord claimed, the process for issuing the notices was automated and they had not been able to pick up the rent cheques from the building.

N5 notices, which in Ontario are notices to end a tenancy for "interfering with others, damage or overcrowding," may also be issued in the course of a renoviction. For example, after tenants refused buyout offers from John Maniatakos and his associates, they received N5 eviction notices for having shoe racks outside their doors in their low-rise building, which they'd had for years. Instead of asking tenants to remove the shoe racks, the landlord issued N5 notices.

N12 notices are also sometimes issued to tenants in the context of renoviction. An N12 notice is a notice to end a tenancy because the landlord or a family member, or a purchaser or their family member, requires the unit. Sometimes a landlord will issue N12 notices either prior to or after issuing N13 notices. Sometimes a landlord will issue N13 notices to some units in a building and N12 notices to other units. Such behaviour simply reinforces the notion that the landlord's primary objective is displacement. Landlords will use the various tools at their disposal, including various types of formal eviction notices, to try to force tenants out of their homes.

HARASSMENT AND INTIMIDATION

If tenants remain in their homes after receiving N13 notices or after persistent informal approaches, landlords may intensify their pressure through harassment and intimidation. In some cases, tenants receive frequent phone calls, texts, or emails about when they are moving out or whether they will accept the latest buyout offer. One tenant said, about the new landlord's repeated buyout offers:

> He started putting a lot of pressure on us. Doing things to annoy us. . . . Lights would be turned off, water would be turned off, without notice. Then more buyout letters would be sent. It was an aggressive tactic to make the building really chaotic and refuse to fix anything, to lure us to take a buyout.

Another way landlords can harass tenants is through frequent unit "inspections" or regularly entering units for other reasons. "Once every two weeks there was an attempt to enter our units for some bogus reason or another. And that just went on and on," said one tenant. Tenants at another building received notices of in-unit inspections twice a week at one point. Often, no one would show up on the day of the inspection. "Usually they don't come, they just send us the email, to intimidate us," said a tenant. The frequent and unpredictable nature of such inspections creates stress for tenants and drives some to move out. Even tenants who have refused to leave their homes for several months may move out as a result of this increased pressure.

Tenants may find repeated buyout offers and frequent intrusions into their home to be intimidating or threatening.

Whether intentionally or not, landlords may create the sense that there will be no end to their efforts or no way for tenants to continue to resist. In extreme cases, a landlord may explicitly threaten tenants in person. Such interactions can happen around the building, which the landlord has free access to, or even inside of a tenant's apartment during an inspection or other interaction. In one case in Toronto, a landlord's associate tried to pressure a senior to move out by repeatedly showing up at her apartment and threatening to have the sheriff come to remove her from her home.

A common intimidation tactic landlords use is lawyers' letters threatening legal action. These are often used if tenants not only remain in their homes but also fight back through collective actions and public campaigns against the landlord. Tenants who deliver letters to their landlords at home or who post information on social media or elsewhere online may receive cease and desist letters from lawyers and other letters threatening prosecution. Landlord lawyers will allege defamation and false accusations, even when tenants carefully stick to the facts and publicly report what is happening at their buildings.

More recently, landlords have sought to criminalize tenant organizing by further threatening the tenancies of organizing tenants, perhaps because they understand that tenants cannot be realistically prosecuted for their actions through criminal or civil proceedings. Tenants in Parkdale who put up banners on their balconies to protest the N13 eviction notices they received were issued N6 eviction notices for "illegal acts." The banners read "Evan Johnsen: Stop the Evictions," and "Neil Spiegel: Stop the Evictions." Similarly, the lawyer for Lankin Investments claimed that tenants fighting renoviction were engaging in conduct "intended to harass, coerce, obstruct and interfere with the Landlord" and that their "Wrongful Conduct" meant they could receive an N6 eviction notice and a fine of up to $50,000, should it continue. While legal experts noted that Lankin's lawyer was interpreting the *Residential Tenancies Act* in novel ways and that, should they move forward with those applications, they would be unlikely to be successful at the LTB, threatening letters don't need to be fully credible to be intimidating.[7]

These types of landlord actions serve to highlight the power imbalance inherent in tenants' struggles to keep their homes in the face of renoviction. There are various avenues open to landlords for taking away a person's shelter via proceedings at the LTB. Tenants have no such power over landlords; they have no ability to throw their landlord into the streets. Recent attempts to criminalize tenant organizing use this threat of losing one's home—perhaps more quickly than through renoviction—to try to discipline tenants.

LIVING IN A CONSTRUCTION ZONE

Landlords may intensify the pressure on tenants who remain in their homes by initiating disruptive renovations within vacant units or in a building's common areas. It is rare that all tenants in a building will resist renoviction for several months. More commonly, some tenants will move out at various stages in the process. Vacant units represent an opportunity for landlords to renovate and raise rents, increasing the value of the building in the process. Vacancies also provide the landlord with the opportunity to further disrupt the lives of tenants who have not moved out. In our experience, landlords renovicting tenants will not renovate common areas of the building unless they succeed in forcing some tenants out of their homes. However, once a certain number of apartments become vacant and the landlord starts renovating those units, they may also initiate renovations of the building's common areas.

Renovations are accompanied by noise, frequent water shutdowns, the lack of hot water, electricity and heat shutdowns, and dust, dirt, and debris. In Toronto, construction noise is permitted from 7 a.m. to 7 p.m. on weekdays and from 9 a.m. to 7 p.m. on Saturday, but these limits are not always respected by landlords. One tenant reported that, "Construction after hours was a big disruption. When they were renovating the unit above mine, there were just guys hammering [after hours]." Even when landlords respect the time restrictions, construction noise can be a nightmare for tenants, particularly people working from home, seniors, and shift workers. One tenant who works from home said, "Even with my door closed my co-workers couldn't hear me [over the construction noise]." When tenants do receive proper notice, daylong water shutdowns to accommodate renovations in vacant units still mean tenants cannot use the washroom, bathe, or sometimes cook for an entire day. But it is not uncommon for such shutdowns to happen without notice, or for the schedule of shutdowns to be changed at the last minute after tenants had received notice. Tenants also frequently report dust, dirt, and construction materials throughout the building while renovations are being done in vacant units or to common areas.

Even if done diligently, completely gutting and remodelling apartments will disrupt the lives of people living in neighbouring units. Landlords seeking to push people out of their homes have an interest in disrupting the lives of tenants who have not yet moved out; thus, there is no incentive for them to be mindful of the comfort and well-being of the remaining tenants. Tenants are not always in a position to determine whether a particular water shutdown is necessary, whether the noise can be minimized, or whether steps could be taken to minimize the various disruptions to their lives caused by the construction; however, tenants often report that they believe their landlords were conducting renovations in a manner that was deliberately more disruptive than necessary. When work continues late into the night and on Sundays, when tenants see vacant units being remodelled but cannot get basic maintenance done in their own unit, or when workers are under the impression that no one is living in the building, it is hard to disagree with tenants' assessments here. All of these conditions simply increase the pressure on tenants to move out.

Buildings where tenants are fighting renoviction can resemble construction zones in other respects as well. Aside from the noise and dust, workers come and go from various apartments, there are materials everywhere, and the front and back doors are usually propped open to facilitate the work or ensure access for workers. These conditions create additional safety concerns for remaining tenants.

At one high-rise building of over a hundred units in Montreal, the landlord succeeded in pushing out the vast majority of tenants by encouraging them to move out ahead of renovations they vowed would be disruptive and then turning the building into a dangerous construction zone. Renovations took place in common areas of the building and within units over the course of months. As tenants moved out, their units would be gutted and extensively renovated, adding to the disruptions faced by remaining tenants. Tenants who remained in their homes faced not only construction noise and dust buildup within their apartments and hazards in hallways and other common areas, but also a lack of hot water, power outages, and the building's heating being shut off ahead of winter.

Occasionally, renovations being done in an adjacent

vacant apartment will cause damage to the apartment of someone who has refused to move out. In one case, a water leak from the apartment above damaged the ceiling in an occupied apartment. Despite there being many workers on site renovating vacant units, the tenant was unable to get their landlord to fix the damage in a timely manner. In another case, a piece of fabric getting stuck in a pipe resulted in sewage coming up from the toilet and bathtub to flood an apartment of a first-floor tenant. Here, Lankin Investments blamed tenants for the sewage backup, noting that a T-shirt was removed from the pipe and telling tenants that "only toilet paper should be flushed down the toilets." Tenants we spoke to reported the more likely cause was that one of the shirts workers place above exposed pipes during plumbing renovations in vacant units accidentally fell into the pipe.

Construction work beyond the confines of individual units may also come with the loss of storage or laundry rooms. Landlords renovicting tenants sometimes seek to add additional apartments to buildings to increase rental revenues, replacing storage or laundry machines that existing tenants rely on.

LEGAL ESCALATION

Finally, a landlord can increase the pressure on tenants to leave their homes by applying to the LTB on the N13 notices that have been issued. If a landlord files an application on an N13, then a hearing will be scheduled where an adjudicator will hear the case. If the adjudicator orders an eviction, the order will include the date on which the sheriff can remove the tenant from their home if they have not already moved out.

Relatively few renovictions make it to this stage. While there has been a significant increase in applications filed by landlords in Ontario on N13 notices, these represent a fraction of renovictions actually taking place.[8]

Notably, even if tenants are successful at a hearing, this does not mean the matter is resolved and their housing is secure. If an adjudicator decides that the renovations the landlord claims they want to carry out do not require vacant possession, there is nothing stopping the landlord from issuing new N13 notices the following day, claiming different renovations. We interviewed tenants from one building who had gone through hearings for two different sets of applications to evict on the basis of N13 notices. Even after the landlord's second applications to evict were denied at a hearing, one tenant said:

> The decision itself didn't touch on the larger questions of good faith, and left the door open [for more N13s]. . . . We didn't lose our homes, but we also didn't get justice. Are we getting N13s tomorrow? Are they appealing? I only feel marginally more secure in my housing than I did before the result of the hearing.

Tenants usually lack the financial resources to pay for legal representation. As a result, there are very few cases where evictions for extensive renovations have been successfully challenged on legal grounds. Tenants who do obtain legal advice and representation on eviction for extensive renovations may be told by legal professionals to move out. With several notable exceptions that we are aware of, the inability of tenants to pay for legal representation, coupled with the lack of positive legal precedents for tenants, has meant that legal professionals are hesitant to litigate renoviction cases. Instead, they will often facilitate displacement by advising tenants to either rely on their right of first refusal or to accept a buyout in exchange for ending their tenancy before their case goes to hearing at the LTB. This is another example of how tenants are very much disadvantaged within the legal eviction process despite having formal equality with landlords under the law.

It is important that tenants know they do not have to move out if they receive an N13 notice and that a landlord does not have the power to simply kick them out of their homes. However, if their landlord is committed to pushing them out, this knowledge alone will not prevent tenants from being pushed out of their homes. Landlords can legally evict tenants on the grounds that they will conduct extensive renovations, and landlords deploy a variety of extralegal tactics to permanently displace tenants.

RENOVICTIONS ARE DYNAMIC SITUATIONS

Discussions of renoviction often focus on supposedly "illegitimate" cases where landlords do not actually intend to renovate or do not intend to conduct very extensive renovations. Such discussions seem to disregard the tenant perspective; we have yet to speak to a tenant who considered their landlord renovicting them to be legitimate. In our view, it is irrelevant whether a landlord actually intends to do the extensive renovations they claim they will carry out and it is a mistake to focus on this issue.[9] Partly, this is because renovictions are dynamic situations where tenants have the ability to alter their landlord's plans. It is also difficult to know what exactly a landlord plans to do at the outset, beyond that they will make some effort to force tenants out of their homes. Some landlords may seek to informally push tenants out but have no intention to issue N13 notices. Some landlords may issue N13 notices but have no intention to ever file eviction applications with the LTB. Some landlords may file eviction applications with the intention to withdraw them if tenants do not move out prior to a hearing and have no intention of obtaining eviction orders at the LTB. Some landlords will try to empty out an entire building but be content to decrease the displacement pressures if they succeed in pushing a certain number of people out. It is not uncommon for a landlord to buy a building, try to force everyone out, succeed partially in this regard, renovate all the vacant units, and quickly sell the building for a profit. Once we drop the pretense that landlords are acting in good faith, all of these possibilities open up. And indeed, landlords display varying levels of commitment to displacing tenants, and certain landlords we have come across seem to deploy only certain tactics.

Meanwhile, how tenants respond to a landlord's attempt to renovict them will necessarily have an impact on the landlord's plans. A landlord may be willing to issue N13 notices, neglect the property, file eviction applications, harass tenants, turn the building into a construction zone, and seek eviction through the LTB, but if tenants move out after being approached informally, then the landlord will not have to use those moves from the playbook. Conversely, a landlord may be willing to do all of these things but back down after issuing N13 notices if tenants fight back and apply enough pressure to the landlord. This does not mean that the landlord did not plan to do those other things or had no actual plans to renovate; rather, tenants succeeded in changing the landlord's plans.

There are landlords like Evan Johnsen and Neil Spiegel, Brendan Riley, and others who have previously pushed tenants out of their homes and conducted extensive renovations before bringing in new tenants at higher rents.[10] These people have demonstrated the willingness and ability to conduct the renovations they claim they will do. But that does not mean that tenants should move out when these landlords issue N13 notices. Tenants who have recently received N13 notices from these landlords have succeeded in fighting back and pressuring their landlords to withdraw the evictions. There is no reason to doubt that the landlords intended to conduct renovations in these cases. But they were only going to conduct these renovations if they succeeded in forcing tenants out of their homes, and that's because renoviction is primarily about displacing tenants, not conducting renovations.

Tenants should not be preoccupied with what their landlord's actual plans are. The most important thing is that they can be certain their landlord's plans do not involve them. Any account or detailed discussion of renoviction that neglects this fact not only fails to accurately capture what is happening across buildings in Toronto and elsewhere, but does tenants a disservice. Once we understand that displacement is the primary objective, it is easy to understand why it is not important to answer whether or not the landlord intends to renovate.

What we do see is that landlords conduct renovations—either extensive or superficial—if they are able to get tenants out of their homes. In almost all renoviction cases, some tenants will move out. And often the landlord will renovate these empty units. But no matter their supposed plans for the other units, we do not see landlords conduct any renovations or extensive repairs inside of units when tenants refuse to move out, even when it seems like it would not be difficult for them to do at least much of the work they proposed while tenants remained in their homes. If we understand renoviction as being primarily about a landlord's desire to conduct renovations, this may seem mysterious.

Now, some may claim that, if the landlord believes the renovations require vacant possession, then of course they will not renovate if tenants do not move out. First, we reiterate that how landlords go about renovicting tenants makes plain that they are not merely trying to conduct renovations they believe require vacant possession in order to be done safely. But even when the LTB has ruled that the renovations the landlord included on their N13 notices could be done without tenants moving out, the renovations have not been done. Furthermore, since some tenants often move out from a building, landlords could, should they desire, temporarily move tenants into vacant units—without terminating anyone's leases—while conducting renovations that genuinely were impossible or unsafe to conduct with someone in the unit. This is not something that we see happen.

The one exception we have seen came after tenants at 1570 Lawrence Avenue West beat Lankin Investments' attempt to renovict them. On the N13 notices issued to tenants, the landlord claimed that "it is mandatory that all main floor units vacate promptly" for plumbing repairs that would take ten to twelve months and involve the removal of "all flooring, walls and kitchens" in the units. As tenants fought back against the evictions, it became clear that one objective for Lankin was the installation of in-suite laundry in newly renovated units throughout the building, which required new pipes to be installed and more extensive work in the first-floor units to connect these pipes to the building's and City's systems. During the eviction hearing for tenants at the building, the landlord provided more information about the specific work required in the first-floor units to install the infrastructure needed to enable in-suite laundry in other units.

After the LTB dismissed Lankin's eviction applications, the landlord decided to go ahead with certain renovations in the first-floor units that tenants remained in. These renovations took less than a couple of months and were narrower in scope than what was noted in the N13s. These renovations also did not upgrade the units tenants remained in, but were done to enable upgrades in other units in the building as those units were vacated, renovated, and rented to new higher-paying tenants. In contrast, after one first-floor tenant moved out upon receiving their N13 notice, their apartment was completely gutted and renovated, then a new tenant was brought in.

THREE

Organizing Against Renoviction

In the face of landlords' renoviction strategy, governments and non-profits have urged tenants to "stay put" and "don't move out."[1] This approach is consistent with their treatment of the landlord renoviction strategy itself which, as we saw in chapter 1, centres the legal aspects of renoviction. Centring the legal aspects obscures the class-conflicted reality of eviction and reinforces a false dichotomy between so-called "illegitimate" and "legitimate" evictions; on the one hand, tenants are susceptible to "illegitimate" eviction when they are unaware of existing legal protections for tenants, on the other hand, there are "legitimate" evictions that tenants must accept. For example, the Canadian Centre for Housing Rights and the National Right to Housing Network tell Ontario tenants:

> Renters . . . can dispute a notice if they don't believe that the landlord intends to do the work. In doing so, they can stay in their home and wait for a possible hearing at the Landlord and Tenant Board (LTB), the legal body that governs disputes between landlords and renters in Ontario. At a hearing, initiated by the landlord's application, the landlord must prove their case for eviction. They must show that the home has to be empty for the renovation to take place.[2]

The practical implication of this view is that once the tenant who faces renoviction learns that an eviction can only be legally enforced after the landlord obtains an order from the LTB, the tenant should simply wait and accept the board's decision. In the meantime, knowledge of the LTB's authority should render the tenant impervious to the landlord's eviction tactics. There are two fundamental problems with this approach.

First, as we discussed in chapter 1, the LTB established with the case of 795 College Street that it has no authority to reinstate a renovicted tenant who wishes to return to their unit once the landlord has rerented the unit to a new tenant. In light of this precedent, it is an absurdity to claim tenants are susceptible to "illegitimate" eviction for lack of knowledge of the legal eviction process and the right of first refusal, while at the same time suggesting tenants wait for and accept the LTB's decision on their landlord's application to evict them for extensive renovations—which, once again, is permitted by law. If the LTB cannot even enforce tenants' supposed right to return to their unit after renovations have been completed, why should tenants consider its authority to evict them to be legitimate?

Second, this approach fails to address landlords' extralegal eviction tactics, which we outlined in chapter 2. Tenants we interviewed told us that landlords' legal, financial, and physical pressure tactics were harmful to them and their neighbours. We are familiar with a number of cases where landlords have succeeded in pushing tenants out of their homes by exerting these forms of pressure. For example, many tenants feel pressured to accept buyouts, and sometimes low-income tenants accept buyouts out of apparent desperation. In one renoviction case in south Etobicoke, the landlord's agent told two tenants with substance use disorders they could take a buyout now or face inevitable eviction later. Believing they had no other option, the tenants accepted buyouts. Within weeks of moving out, these tenants were reportedly staying at a homeless shelter.

When tenants do hold out against renoviction, landlords' extralegal tactics are nonetheless damaging. In Ottawa, a landlord began disruptive renovations in a row of rooming houses and boarded up windows and fire escape doors as if the building had been condemned. At a building in Hamilton, the landlord shut the water off for three months at the same time as filing evictions for extensive renovations against tenants and appealed to delay the enforcement of City orders. The landlord of two working women roommates living above a storefront in north Toronto had one of their vehicles towed after he issued multiple different eviction notices to them and they refused to move out. At another building in north Toronto, because the new landlord refused to fix the building's broken washing machines for over a year, tenants had no other option but to travel off-site to do their laundry, leaving seniors to haul their laundry by hand to the nearest laundromat more than half a kilometre away. A Parkdale tenant we interviewed told us that when her building sold, the new landlord insisted on refusing cash rent payments and was quick to issue eviction notices for non-payment of rent against tenants who did not pay by other means. As a result, she had to accompany her neighbour, an elderly disabled man, to the bank to purchase a bank draft because he no longer understood how to make his rent payments and could have been evicted as a result. Another tenant described the impact of landlords' extralegal eviction tactics this way:

> It takes up all your mental energy. So much of your life revolves around your housing situation. The landlord has so much power. Knowing that the landlord is lying

> to get you out, it feels like you're fighting an uphill battle. It's so drawn out. You have to live with it for months. Dealing with the landlord's paralegals, construction guys, it puts a lot of stress on you. It's anxiety inducing.

Clearly, as these examples suggest, tenants will not necessarily be able to resist the various pressure tactics landlords use as part of their renoviction strategy through a better understanding of the legal eviction process alone.

If better knowledge of the law does not serve to protect tenants from renoviction, how do tenants create the conditions under which they can develop the collective capacity to withstand landlords' attempts to renovict them? Faced with landlords attempting to push them out of their homes, why shouldn't tenants fight back to keep their homes? Working-class tenants across Toronto, and in cities throughout Ontario, have had success by organizing at the level of their rental apartment buildings, and in some cases, at the level of renter districts. Understanding that their landlords were simply seeking to displace them, tenants have organized to fight evictions directly and in the most effective ways they can. Before we offer some observations on the content of these tenants' organizing initiatives, we need to critically assess how governments and non-profits treat tenant organizing.

Governments and non-profits do not discuss organizing as a process through which tenants develop their collective capacities. Instead, they present non-profit advocacy organizations as possessors of expertise, funds, and political influence that individual tenants need access to. For example, according to a recent report from Right to Housing Toronto, "The success of eviction prevention measures is also contingent on a network of community legal clinics, other legal housing organizations, housing advocates and tenant support groups who build tenants' awareness of their rights and obligations."[3]

If eviction prevention depends on the work of non-profit organizations, then tenants cannot expect to stop evictions through independent organizing. The City of Toronto takes a similar approach. An early version of the City's eviction prevention handbook suggests tenants speak to their Tenant Association. This suggestion assumes the tenant lives in one of the relatively few buildings in Toronto where there is an active organization of tenants. It also presents Tenant Associations as yet another institution that tenants may access as a service user. A more recent version of the handbook frames things similarly and encourages tenants to speak to a Tenant Association near them.[4] Absent from the information the City provides tenants are any examples of how Toronto tenants have acted collectively to resist renoviction.

When non-profits present tenant organizing as something more than service provision, they portray it as tenant engagement with the legal eviction process, or as the work of organizations external to tenants themselves. In a recent report on renovictions in Toronto, non-profit advocacy group ACORN presents two renoviction case studies.[5] In both cases, the report depicts tenants disputing landlords' eviction applications at LTB hearings as examples of tenant organizing. In the first case, we learn that a group of Etobicoke tenants received a grant from the City of Toronto to help cover their legal fees. In the second case, the landlord at an east-end Toronto building succeeded in renovicting the tenants living there. The report's presentation of these cases as examples of tenant organizing reduces the potential for collective action to tenant participation in the legal process of eviction and calls into question its claim that, "If not for the ACORN Tenant Union calling out cases in our city, landlords would be able to quietly displace tenants and face no recourse."[6]

In chapter 1, we said renoviction is a landlord strategy to increase rents and property values. In chapter 2, we outlined the landlord playbook of tactics to remove tenants from rental units. What we wish to emphasize here is that a critical component of the landlord renoviction strategy and playbook of tactics is to maintain or increase the existing separation between tenants living in a building so as to eliminate tenant opposition to renoviction. In the most sophisticated approaches to renoviction, landlords avoid uniform communication with all tenants in a building and insist on only communicating with tenants individually about buyouts and/or threats of eviction, as the case may be. Landlords are apparently conscious of the need to keep tenants separated when, for example, instead of issuing N13 eviction notices to all tenants in the building at once and risking the unification of tenants around a shared threat of eviction, they restrain themselves and target a smaller number of specific tenants with eviction notices while maintaining generalized pressure on all tenants through various means.

ORGANIZING EARLY

Organizing is a process through which working-class people develop their politics and organizational strength by collectively confronting bosses, landlords, and the state. By organizing, working-class people build independent organizations capable of taking direct action in their own interests. Organizing is distinct from public advocacy and lobbying that attempt to integrate working-class grievances into the state. Toronto tenants have increasingly turned to organizing at their buildings and renter districts to stop renovictions. When tenants organize, they establish independent methods of communication, collective decision-making, and action in their own interests as tenants. Organizing, in our view, does not mean that tenants set up organizational structures, such as elected executives, which only tend to concentrate activity and decision-making among a small minority. Rather, organizing involves the greatest possible number of tenants. At its most basic, organizing means that tenants talk to their neighbours at their building, share information, and begin to make decisions together about how to act as a group to improve their conditions.

As we have seen, the sale of a building is a moment in time when tenants are likely to experience displacement pressure. In this moment, it is critical for tenants to make timely interventions within their building. The sooner all tenants become aware of the sale of the building and can anticipate the potential for renoviction, the better, because it gives tenants more time to organize ahead of the landlord implementing their renoviction strategy. If not at the point of sale, the sooner that tenants start organizing, the better.

Tenants we interviewed who organized to stop renovictions at their buildings benefited from establishing methods of communication with their neighbours, including regular group meetings, one-on-one conversations, and app-based chat groups. Often, tenants begin by having informal conversations with neighbours they already know, or by approaching neighbours they don't know in the hallway, entranceway, or parking lot. Through these informal talks, tenants discuss the situation at the building and acknowledge each other's concerns. Thus tenants confirm to one another that they are living under shared conditions and that the landlord is acting against their interests as tenants. Once two or more tenants have reached this baseline understanding together, they have started to organize.

A particularly proactive tenant we interviewed described reaching out to neighbours after her new landlord sent notices to all tenants claiming the landlord planned to renovate their buildings and encouraging tenants to accept buyouts:

> I just started knocking on doors when I got the notice, first in my building, then neighbouring buildings. The reactions I got from my neighbours about wanting to stay and not take a deal gave me confidence to go further and keep talking to neighbours. And a couple of other tenants started helping out.

Similarly, a Hamilton tenant and his partner learned their building was for sale and immediately reached out to their neighbours door to door. The tenant we interviewed was motivated to fight a possible renoviction because he had been evicted for landlord's own use from his last three apartments and because he was aware that renoviction had become more common in the city. The couple gathered important information while canvassing their neighbours. Some of their neighbours had lived in the building for decades and paid rents that were a third of average market rent in the city. These tenants were especially worried about the threat of eviction posed by the potential sale and were willing to organize to defend their homes if it came to that.

The next step tenant organizers usually take is to call a meeting, open to all tenants, typically in a common area of the building—entranceway, hallway or landing, parking lot—to discuss the situation as a building of tenants. This initial meeting is often crucial because it is the first time tenants establish building-wide communication among themselves. At a well-attended building meeting, tenants are in a position to decide collectively to fight to remain in their homes.

Once this decision is taken, tenants are wise to agree on how they will reach out to neighbours who did not attend the first meeting and stay in contact with each other between now and the next meeting. Tenant organizers reach out to neighbours who were absent from the first building meeting through already-existing social networks within the building or by knocking on neighbours' doors. To stay in contact between meetings, a common method is for tenants to create an app-based group chat for tenants in the building, for example, using WhatsApp. From there, tenants can hold regular meetings to make decisions and divide up tasks about responding to communication from the landlord, developing their own demands, and putting the landlord on notice of their demands. Between meetings, tenants may continue to share updates and other information over the building group chat. Two tenants we interviewed from the same building described how increased communication among their neighbours allowed them to coordinate their opposition to the landlord's extralegal eviction tactic of frequent unit inspections:

> We had the group chat, where everyone shared information. If the landlord was coming in the building, we would let each other know and protect each other.

> The first time we defied them and denied them entry to our units, it was during the pandemic. I was nervous, standing behind my door, looking at my phone, and reading, "They're here, they're at the back door."

Organizing early allows tenants to mitigate against the landlord targeting and pushing out individual tenants in the initial stages of renoviction. When the landlord succeeds in rapidly removing a number of tenants from a building with extralegal eviction tactics early on, it diminishes the potential for tenants to organize effectively. Just as each unit the landlord succeeds in vacating increases their rate of rent extraction, each eviction tenants prevent depresses that rate and strengthens the organizing position of tenants in the building as a whole. It is only by organizing that tenants counteract the tendency toward their separation in the rental housing market and by the landlord.

At one building, tenants formed an organization immediately after learning their building had been sold. Throughout the first year after the change in ownership, the new landlord relied on buyouts, removing the live-in superintendent, neglecting maintenance, and making it difficult for some tenants to pay their rent by refusing to accept cash payments and no longer physically collecting rent payments at the building. More than a year later, the landlord issued N13 notices for extensive renovations to all tenants in the building. By this time, tenants had already established a building-based organization with months of experience collectivizing grievances around maintenance and disrepair and rent payment issues. Having developed collective practices in opposition to the new landlords' extralegal eviction strategies, the tenants were in a strong position to fight the landlord's N13 notices. Tenants launched a public campaign against the renovictions, and within months the landlord conceded and withdrew the N13 notices.[7]

Tenants we interviewed said that organizing with their neighbours made them feel less isolated and lessened the negative psychological and emotional consequences of being subjected to renoviction. One tenant who successfully organized with her neighbours to stop renovictions at her building told us that before the renoviction fight, she had not known the other tenants in her building, but since beating renoviction, they've started celebrating holidays together. In this sense, organizing is the antidote to the despair tenants often feel when landlords threaten to kick them out of their homes. One tenant we spoke with shared that the positive difference that organizing with neighbours has made in his partner's life is "the bright side" of facing renoviction.

NON-RELIANCE ON LEGAL STRATEGY

We have discussed how the legal process of eviction for extensive renovations is designed to sanction and enforce renoviction. Therefore, it is not surprising that tenant organizing is most effective when it starts before the landlord initiates the legal eviction process and when it does not abide by the legal eviction process once it is underway. Organizing is a rational response to renoviction, whether or not the landlord has issued N13 notices to tenants. Tenants faced with renoviction who wish to remain in their homes should act accordingly.

We conducted extensive interviews with twenty-five tenants who have faced or are currently facing renoviction. Nineteen of the tenants we interviewed beat their renovictions. Eleven of these tenants who beat their renovictions did so by organizing with their neighbours to increase the financial, social, and emotional costs on their landlords to the point where their landlords withdrew the evictions before they ended up at hearings in front of the LTB. Five other tenants we interviewed won their cases at the LTB after their and their neighbours' organizing efforts did not result in the landlord withdrawing the evictions. Three tenants resisted their landlords' informal approaches and extralegal tactics and did not receive N13 eviction notices. Four tenants, at one building, were evicted by the LTB. The remaining two tenants interviewed continue to organize with their neighbours against their landlords' ongoing attempt to renovict them.

The success of organized tenants can be attributed, in part, to the decision of their building committees to not rely on the legal process to protect them from renoviction. Instead of focusing on preparing for the possibility of a future LTB hearing, tenants proactively and directly confronted their landlords, demanding a stop to the renovictions before their cases ended up at the LTB. For some of the tenants we interviewed, organizing to directly challenge the landlord was intuitive. Other tenants told us that before they themselves faced renoviction, and before looking into how other Toronto tenants have been fighting renoviction, they had assumed Ontario landlord-tenant law protected tenants from renoviction: "It was interesting to know how many people are fighting back and that the LTB may not save us. That was scary and sad. It felt uncomfortable. It felt like we had to take matters into our own hands."

In renoviction cases where landlords issue N13s and file eviction applications with the LTB, organized tenants are more likely to be able to stay in their homes than tenants who do not organize with their neighbours. In one case in Parkdale, tenants renting in a five-unit house received N13 notices. The tenants organized, refused to move out, and delivered a demand letter to their landlord at his home, but the landlord filed eviction applications with the LTB anyway. However, upon realizing there were technical defects in the N13 notices, the landlord withdrew the applications on the day of the board hearing. The landlord's legal representative threatened to issue new N13s to the tenants, but more than a year later, tenants still have not received new eviction notices.

In another case in north Toronto, tenants organized an escalating campaign of actions against their landlord that did not result in the landlord withdrawing the eviction applications before the hearings, but tenants ended up winning their case at the LTB. Tenants told us that the months of organizing together enabled them to withstand their landlord's renoviction tactics and coordinate their defence at the LTB hearings.[8] Tenants honoured their commitments to each other and collectively refused to move out despite the landlord's multiple buyout offers, legal threats, and neglect of repairs and maintenance. They also worked together to gather evidence, prepare testimony, and retain legal representation in advance of the eviction hearings, coordinate their schedules and transportation to attend the hearings virtually as a group from a local community centre, and during the hearings, supported each other through having to provide emotional testimony and endure antagonistic cross-examination by the landlord's legal representative.

In contrast, in cases that we are familiar with where tenants have not organized but have taken their cases as far as the LTB hearing, they have often agreed to move out in exchange for buyout offers or more time to find a new place, or have had the LTB rule against them and order eviction.

From our interviews, we learned that many tenants, in the course of organizing with their neighbours against renoviction, developed their analysis of how the political and legal state apparatuses sanction the landlord strategy of renoviction. Rooming house tenants in Ottawa facing renoviction learned the City of Ottawa was on their landlord's side. Smart Living Properties bought a row of rooming houses with more than one hundred units at 146–170 Osgoode Street and attempted to renovict the tenants, turning the buildings into a construction site through disruptive renovations. Some tenants contacted the City of Ottawa and local politicians hoping these authorities would intervene on the tenants' behalf. Instead, while the landlord worked to push tenants out, the City of Ottawa issued orders prohibiting occupancy in the buildings based on alleged fire safety issues and sent social workers, police officers, and fire department officials to the buildings to pressure tenants to move out.

In the case of one building where tenants beat renoviction by organizing, the local MPP from the New Democratic Party (NDP) reached out to tenants after early media coverage of their campaign. The tenants agreed to meet with the MPP, who assured them of his support. Later, the MPP's office informed the group that it had held a meeting with the landlord without them. The MPP's office had not notified the actual people facing eviction of this meeting in advance, let alone invited them to attend the meeting. The MPP's office told the tenants that at the closed-door meeting, at the MPP's urging, the landlord had agreed to increase the amount of money it was prepared to pay tenants to move out. Reflecting on her experience organizing against renoviction, one organizer explained how her worldview changed:

> I learned a lot. I changed my mind about the place of institutions in my life and my reliance on them, or the idea that they protect me. I don't have that feeling anymore. I learned how powerful a very small group of people can be, if they all agree and stick together. It's unbelievably powerful. It's fragile, incredibly fragile, so if you have that coalition, if you've got it, work to keep it.

TURNING IT AROUND ON LANDLORDS

The landlord strategy of renoviction rests on forms of legal, financial, and physical pressure applied on tenants to push them out of their homes. In response, tenants have found ways to exert their own forms of organized, collective pressure on landlords to stop renovictions. These forms of organized, collective pressure have included using poster and flyer campaigns to publicize their fights against renoviction in their own neighbourhoods and in other buildings owned by the same landlord, holding protests and other actions targeting their landlords' businesses, directly confronting their landlords and agents of their landlords at their buildings and homes, and speaking out publicly against renoviction in the media and on social media.

One tenant told us that her committee's media strategy was to use media coverage to put pressure on the landlord by naming him in public:

> The first time CP24 came by and asked some of us what was happening at the building, we made sure his name was put out there. The reporter attempted to contact him. He replied to the reporter saying she should be careful of how she portrays his views, be careful what she puts out there. But she still put the story out. That was fun. It was fun to watch him suffer.

In another campaign, locals from different buildings supported their neighbours facing renoviction by distributing posters and flyers throughout the neighbourhood about their fight. The posters and flyers encouraged renters in the area to email the landlords to demand a stop to the evictions and included a QR code that linked to a template email anyone could adapt and send. That QR code was accessed nearly one thousand times. Meanwhile, a pair of tenants from one Toronto building distributed flyers in their neighbourhood encouraging their neighbours to call their landlord and an investor in their building to demand the N13 notices issued to them be withdrawn. The plan for the phone zap was also shared on social media.

Tenants told us they were able to apply pressure on their landlords by targeting the landlord's other, unrelated business interests. In one case, tenants facing renoviction were joined by neighbours from other buildings in delivering a demand letter to a restaurant franchise owned by their landlord. The action got the attention of the franchiser, who did not want any further negative publicity, and pressured the franchisee to withdraw the evictions against his tenants.

> We met at Tim Hortons, a whole bunch of us. Must have been fifteen people. We went to his restaurant and we had a big sign that said "no eviction." We gave a letter to one of the cashiers to give to the landlord. We took a photo and we put it on Facebook.

In another case, affected families held an informational picket on the sidewalk outside the storefront business of their landlord's wife. Tenants distributed flyers with a photo of the smiling couple on it informing patrons about the proprietor's association with the ongoing renovictions at their building. Before leaving, they decorated the storefront with colourful protest signs created by their children. One sign depicted a stick figure family with two pet cats standing in front of their building under a shining yellow sun. The caption read, "This is my grandma, my mommy, and my home. Stop the renoviction!! Help my family thrive." Soon after this action, tenants received a message from another business owner who shared space with their landlord's wife at her storefront location. She told tenants she was so disturbed to learn what was happening to them that she had decided to sever ties with their landlord's wife, and she wished them the best of luck in their fight. Tenants later learned that this action caused their landlord a serious enough domestic problem that it contributed to his decision to no longer pursue renoviction against them.

Many of the tenants we interviewed got together with their neighbours to deliver demand letters to their landlords' personal residences. This is a reasonable course of action to take considering that, more often than not, landlords who use the renoviction strategy do not provide tenants with their contact information or business addresses. Even in cases where the landlord does provide contact information, it makes sense that tenants would present themselves at their landlord's home while the landlord tries to displace them from their own homes. We repeatedly heard from people we interviewed that they appreciated the proportionality of these landlord home visits, since their landlord or agents habitually confronted them at theirs.

A group of tenants visited their landlord at his exurban mansion in the Greater Toronto Area. A few of the tenants went to knock on the door while most of the group remained on the sidewalk. The landlord came to the door, furious, demanding tenants leave immediately. The delegation explained they needed to meet with him as a group to discuss having him withdraw the eviction applications he had filed against them. When the landlord said this was the wrong place for a meeting, tenants pointed out that he had ignored their recent letter. At this point, the landlord's wife came outside to see what the heated exchange was about. The presence of his wife only further agitated the landlord, who shouted at her, in front of his unexpected guests, to go back inside the house. Since then, this landlord has refrained from issuing N13 eviction notices at new buildings his firm acquires.

Another tenant committee held a protest outside their landlord's home after they knocked and he refused to come to the door. On a Sunday afternoon, tenants stood on the sidewalk outside their landlord's house on an upscale residential street in east Toronto, chanting "Stop the evictions." Tenants took turns leading chants on a megaphone; one parent's three-year-old daughter insisted on taking her turn too. The protesters also handed out flyers about the renoviction to their landlord's neighbours who were returning from walking the dog or who came out to the street to see what all the noise was about. Tenants chanted for around fifteen minutes before the landlord finally showed his face, stepping out on his front porch to address them from a distance. At first, he tried to reproach tenants for scaring his two young children inside with their noise, but he was shouted down. The small crowd confronted him about evicting their young children from their homes. They said they would stop making noise when he agreed to withdraw the N13 notices he had issued. And he committed to withdrawing the N13s, right then and there. Although this was not to be the end of the renoviction fight, these tenants were ultimately successful, and actions like this one showed them what they were capable of accomplishing as a group.

A single father renting above a storefront in west-end Toronto received an N13 that stated his landlord, a board member of a well-known charity in the city, planned to demolish his washroom. One Sunday morning, he and a small group of friends and supporters met around the corner from where his landlord lived. The group walked over to the landlord's house and the tenant rang the doorbell. The landlord's wife answered the door. She was polite and seemed surprised to learn about the eviction notice her husband had issued. The tenant left her with a letter stating that if the landlord did not withdraw the N13 within one week, he was prepared to make the eviction a more public issue. Two days later, the tenant received an email from the landlord that read: "We still believe that the best way to do the work is a complete renovation with the apartment vacant but considering your disagreement you'll be happy to hear that we will not be pursuing the LTB hearing and will work with our contractor to effect the repairs with the minimal amount of work and impact on the apartment."

INTERPRETING TENANTS' EXHORTATION TO "KNOW YOUR RIGHTS"

When we asked tenants what they thought other tenants should know about fighting renoviction, many replied "know your rights." This interested us, especially in light of the fact that the majority of the people we interviewed beat their renoviction through extralegal means: their landlords withdrew from evicting them without their cases ever going in front of the LTB. If tenants succeeded in beating renoviction by organizing and raising the social, financial, and emotional costs for landlords to proceed with their renoviction strategy, and therefore, by not relying on a legal strategy to stop renoviction, what explains tenants' frequent insistence on the importance of knowing your rights?

After being notified by their landlord that they would have to move out, and before forming an organization at their building to fight the renoviction, two tenants from one building described themselves as being in a state of not knowing their rights:

> We needed a stepping stone . . . we didn't know our rights. We were talking about packing up and trying to

> find something. I cried that night. I can't believe this is happening. I know the apartment is not mine . . . it was frustrating.

> All of us were in that boat, we didn't fully know our rights . . . I thought we would have to go to the LTB to fight this. That was the biggest perspective change for me, trusting in institutions, they are not there for us. That was eye-opening.

After forming an organization at their building and waging a more than year-long campaign that succeeded in stopping the renovictions, a tenant quoted above offers some insight into how she came to know her rights:

> I learned to reach out and just know your rights because honestly, if I didn't know better, if I didn't know what we're capable of, I would have moved elsewhere with three times the rent. Reach out. You have community around you. Reach out to neighbours. Know who you are going up against. Find out who they are. Stick together as a community.

In such contexts, we have to interpret tenants' exhortation to "know your rights" to mean much more than knowledge of Ontario landlord-tenant law. As we saw above, governments and non-profits attribute "illegitimate" evictions to tenants' lack of awareness of their legal rights. When their message to tenants is to "know your rights," they are suggesting that tenants should learn to distinguish between legitimate and illegitimate eviction, while offering nothing to tenants who wish to oppose their landlord's renoviction strategy. By contrast, when tenants who have organized and effectively opposed their landlords say other tenants should know their rights, they do not mean rights in the narrow, legal sense. The tenant quoted above explicitly framed "rights" as a function of the development of her and her fellow tenants' collective capacities. Other tenants we interviewed who urged tenants to "know their rights" expressed similar sentiments. Therefore, we should understand tenants' frequent reference to "rights" to mean tenants' collective practice of asserting control over the spaces they inhabit but do not own as property, against property owners and the legal system that guarantees their private property. Understood in this way, when tenants we interviewed who organized to fight renoviction say "know your rights," this is not merely advice to familiarize oneself with landlord-tenant law but a call for tenants to organize against dispossession.

DISTRICT-BASED ORGANIZING

In 2022, tenants at 12 Lansdowne Avenue in Parkdale organized to beat renoviction and, more recently, tenants in a few low-rise buildings along Keele Street in north Toronto have organized to push back against their landlords' attempts to renovict them.[9] In these cases, tenants organized early because there was district-based organizing established in the neighbourhood—Parkdale Organize in the former case, and the Keele Area Tenant Committee in the latter. Both Parkdale Organize and KATC aim to build working-class power in their respective districts. They intervene within specific areas of the city with significant amounts of rental housing, and over the years, they have developed considerable experience in struggles against landlords.[10] In our view, these groups have worked to make independent working-class organizing more commonplace in Parkdale and the Keele area, as greater numbers of working-class people in those districts come to view organizing as a viable way to improve their lives. Here we will give a detailed account of how KATC has contributed to the development of independent organizing in the Keele area. We base this section on our ongoing involvement with KATC, an in-depth interview with a founding member of KATC, and KATC newsletters.

For the past few years, KATC has organized along a four-kilometre stretch of Keele Street in north Toronto and in nearby buildings. The group grew out of campaigns against renovictions at different buildings in the neighbourhood and has since gone on to support tenants organizing at their own buildings against evictions, disrepair, harassment, and above guideline rent increases. KATC has been able to intervene early in cases of renoviction along Keele Street due to its presence and activity in the area.

The struggle against renoviction at 2419 Keele Street catalyzed organizing against renovictions in the Keele area. In 2021, Brendan Riley and his partners acquired 2419 Keele Street and issued N13 eviction notices to all the tenants in the twelve-unit building. By that time, Riley's firm had already acquired and renovated, or was in the process of renovating, a few other low-rise buildings in Toronto. Low interest rates during the early stages of the COVID-19 pandemic increased the volume of cheap credit available to real estate investors, accelerating trends that began in the 2010s. Investors used the opportunity to buy up apartment buildings and further consolidate ownership of rental housing in Canadian cities. In Toronto, investors were actively purchasing buildings in areas with high concentrations of low-income, disproportionately racialized renters paying low rents, where they anticipated land values to rise. Low- and medium-rise buildings in inner-suburban areas in Etobicoke, North York, and Scarborough were changing hands, and in many cases the new owners attempted to renovict tenants. While workers bore the brunt of COVID-19 infections, landlords increased their wealth by displacing these same workers from their homes.

Along the stretch of Keele Street intersecting the 401 highway, there are many low-rise buildings similar to 2419 Keele Street. These are the sort of apartment buildings that are accessible to the individual owners, partnerships, and small real estate firms that typically deploy the renoviction strategy. With transit projects and large developments promising to increase property values in the area, and with rents rapidly increasing in Canadian cities well beyond the downtown cores, there was (and still is) a lot of money to be made by buying up these buildings and pushing out long-term tenants.

In 2022, after tenants at 2419 Keele Street had defeated their landlords' renoviction attempt and saw the N13 eviction notices issued to them withdrawn, investors purchased other buildings in the area and began trying to renovict tenants. Tenants we had made contact with set up meetings at these buildings, including 1570 Lawrence Avenue West, and tenants from 2419 Keele Street joined the meetings. Drawing from their recent success, tenants talked about how their landlord had tried to push them out and how they'd organized to keep their homes. For the tenants facing eviction, their neighbours from just down the street were a welcome sight. Here was living proof that people like them could stop renovictions. Tenants from 2419 Keele Street were also keen to share lessons learned from their recent struggle. For them, beating renoviction at their own building was not enough while landlords were renovicting their neighbours at nearby buildings. "I was nervous and inexperienced, but it was also very exciting," remembered one tenant who spoke at these meetings. "We had a lot of agency and I wanted that for other people."

Within months, fourteen tenants from these buildings met at the local public library to discuss what they saw happening in their neighbourhood. By this time, these tenants had not only gained experience organizing to challenge renovictions and unacceptable housing conditions at their own buildings, but many of them had already been actively supporting their neighbours living nearby. They agreed they needed to warn other tenants in the area about the threat of renoviction and, more importantly, they wanted to show their neighbours what they could do to stop landlords. One tenant reflected back on that moment in time: "There were discussions about turning these different committees into a network that could build momentum and support each other. Demonstrations and talking to other tenants had become part of my routine. Keeping that momentum up was important to me."

Tenants at the meeting intended to organize with fellow renters in their district but initially struggled to define the area. Tenants agreed that they lived in North York—an administrative district of the City of Toronto covering nearly 177 square kilometres. However, the four-kilometre stretch of Keele Street tenants lived along or near to, bounded by Sheppard Avenue West in the north and Lawrence Avenue West in the south, runs through multiple electoral ridings, wards, and officially recognized neighbourhoods. The tenants' formal inclusion in different electoral districts or official Toronto neighbourhoods seemed to obscure what they all shared in common as working-class renters. One tenant at the meeting offered additional insight. She said the absence of any local working-class organization had made their area practically illegible. "If we are having a hard time defining the area, maybe it is because there is something missing from the place we live and we have to do something about it."[11] Her neighbours agreed and they decided to do something about it together.

The newly formed KATC planned a public meeting for working-class people in the area to learn from KATC members about how they could organize against landlords at their own buildings. In the lead-up, KATC members dropped over two thousand flyers under unit doors in buildings in the area. Around sixty tenants turned out for the meeting in the basement of the local library. The message from KATC speakers was simple and direct: landlords are trying to push working-class people out of our homes, no one is coming to save us, and the best way to defend ourselves is to organize with our neighbours at our buildings. KATC then invited attendees to speak from the front of the room about the situation at their buildings. Numerous speakers came forward from buildings where landlords were trying to push tenants out.

After the public meeting, KATC members reached out to attendees and encouraged them to hold meetings at their buildings. Other tenants from the area who hadn't attended the meeting at the library also reached out using the contact info on the meeting flyer—in some cases tenants called months after receiving the flyer—and KATC members encouraged them to hold meetings at their own buildings. These initial building meetings, attended by KATC members, resulted in committees being formed by tenants at various buildings in the area. In turn, some of these organizers from building committees have become KATC members and began to support other tenants in the area.

KATC has worked to support tenants and develop the power of working-class people in the area. The volunteer-run group is not an organization made up of building representatives, nor does it direct the work of a few handpicked or self-appointed tenants from buildings in the area. Unlike many tenant unions or non-profits like ACORN that prioritize signing up dues-paying members, KATC supports new organizers whether or not they become members. Its aim is more in line with the principle of self-organization: to support organizers in forming committees composed of many tenants at their buildings. KATC thus emphasizes the importance of involving the greatest possible number of tenants at a building. The real or perceived reluctance of tenants to get involved sometimes frustrates new organizers, who may begin to question whether their efforts are worthwhile. KATC members encourage patience and diligence, advising organizers to work methodically to enable the broadest possible participation from their neighbours, to plan meetings at times when most neighbours are available, and to use each meeting as an opportunity to engage neighbours in concrete actions. These actions can be as simple as tenants signing a demand letter or committing to confront the landlord at a specific date and time. Through this work, KATC members build long-term political relationships with new organizers: tenants who take the initiative to bring neighbours together at their buildings to make collective decisions about how to address their issues.

Most new organizers have not faced renoviction before. Many have no prior organizing experience. At times, organizers are under the mistaken impression that landlords' power to run their properties as they see fit is incontestable. "One of the barriers is that people think you can't confront your landlord collectively," explained a KATC member. "I tell them that we did it at my building and it worked. That is the number one thing that cuts through the noise." New organizers may also wrongly assume that the law or politicians will protect them from renoviction. KATC members clarify that tenants are up against both predatory landlords and the institutionalized force of the state that facilitates displacement. They explain that looking to the letter of the law or to support from politicians is more likely to get tenants evicted than to keep them in their homes. For KATC, the illusions that non-profits perpetuate about renoviction and how to resolve issues with landlords keep tenants powerless and must therefore be smashed.

At the same time, KATC offers emotional support to new organizers. From bitter experience, KATC members know the emotional toll renoviction takes. Members pride themselves on showing up for their neighbours when called upon. "[KATC] is like a family because we are people who can trust and rely on each other. I love to guide, comfort, and support my neighbours who are struggling."[12] Members reassure new organizers that they are not going away; they will continue to be present at meetings with their neighbours and back them in confrontations with their landlords.

Once a tenant committee is established, the committee intervenes in struggles as they arise at the building. Tenants at buildings in the area have organized in response to lack of maintenance, harassment from the landlord, rent increases, and evictions and informal eviction threats, including renovictions. Tenants have delivered collective letters to their landlords at their offices, other businesses, and homes, and have engaged in collective direct action to raise the social and financial costs to their landlords, with varying degrees of success. Through this organizing work, tenants at buildings in the area build up their capacities and their power, putting them in a better position to address issues in the future.

At one building, tenants successfully fought back against harassment, lack of heating and maintenance, and evictions for having air conditioners. The building committee remained active, and when an elderly woman who has lived at the building for over forty years received an eviction notice after her son confronted the property manager over repeatedly entering her unit without her permission, her neighbours had her back. After she received the notice alleging that her son had impaired the safety of the property manager, she knocked on an organizer's door. The organizer assured her that she had his and the committee's support and called a meeting. At the meeting, the committee decided to get as many neighbours as possible to call and email the landlord on the same day demanding she withdraw the eviction. Many tenants made the calls and sent the emails. The landlord withdrew the eviction within a week.[13]

Where there are social divisions between tenants at a building—for example, based on language barriers—KATC draws on the language skills of tenants there and of its own membership to overcome those divisions. Language skills are especially valuable in the early stages of organizing at a building when it is crucial to bridge such divides. Many tenants in the Keele area are Spanish, Tagalog, and Turkish speakers, and KATC members and contacts speak these languages. This allows the group to provide interpretation at meetings and translate texts into relevant languages. Informal one-on-one and small group conversations between bilingual KATC members and tenants who share the same first language supplement larger group meetings held in English. In one instance, a bilingual organizer from a building took the initiative to invite all the Spanish-speaking families to a meeting held in Spanish, after newcomers to Canada who received eviction notices feared the evictions would hurt their chances of remaining in the country. One family had moved out for this reason after receiving the notice. At the Spanish-language meeting, tenants received his message: an eviction is not a criminal matter that affects one's immigration status, and no one has to move out.

KATC's hallmark is its ongoing physical presence in the Keele area. Because KATC members live in the area, members can have regular, informal conversations with local people about organizing. One KATC member takes his wife to church on Sundays. One Sunday, while socializing with congregants after church, he met several tenants from a nearby building complex. They told him that conditions at their buildings were deteriorating due to the landlord ignoring their repair requests. The member spoke to them about organizing and gave them copies of a KATC newsletter. These tenants later reported that word of this discussion got back to the building superintendent and made their landlord more responsive to their repair requests in the future. KATC members once attended the picket line of striking grocery store workers in the area. Months later, some tenants facing eviction from a rented house off Keele Street contacted KATC. They explained that they had heard about the group from their grocery store worker friend who had met KATC members on the picket line. These are only two notable examples. KATC members regularly discuss their organizing and share flyers and newsletters with other tenants in plaza parking lots, coffee shops, laundromats, and convenience stores in the area. Unlike many non-profits and advocacy groups, KATC engages with working-class people in its area and does not rely on online communications to advance a reformist agenda.

Its ongoing presence in the area is also what enables KATC to intervene early on in cases of renoviction or potential renoviction. As discussed, organizing early is crucial to stopping landlords from pushing out individual tenants in the initial stages of renoviction. The more tenants who remain in their homes, the stronger the position of all tenants. Because KATC has contacts in buildings in the area, has distributed flyers and newsletters to buildings in the area, is aware of what is happening in the area, and has members who socialize with tenants in the area, the group often finds out about renovictions or is contacted by tenants early.

In early 2025, KATC held a second public meeting at the local library, flyering thousands of apartments in the lead-up, including putting flyers under doors at 2866 Keele Street. "In February, we got a KATC flyer about a meeting at the library," explained one tenant from the building who has since become an organizer at her building. "My neighbour and I decided to go. When we got there, we saw other tenants from our building! We were all thinking the same thing. At the meeting, we talked to a KATC member who told us to hold a meeting at our building."[14] Tenants at the building were being pressured by the landlord to move out for renovations. The organizer and her neighbours went on to confront their landlord in response to these attempts to renovict them, showing up as a group at her home and at her office and collectively refusing to move out.[15] This new organizer has also shown interest in supporting other tenants in the area. "I did not expect to receive this kind of support in Canada where everyone is busy. What KATC is doing is different. Having this support has made me strong."

Weeks after the public meeting, tenants from two other low-rise buildings along Keele Street—2548 and 2550—contacted KATC. Although tenants from the buildings had not attended the meeting at the library, they had received the flyers with KATC's contact information. The tenants reported that their buildings had recently been sold. Since the sale, an agent of the landlord had repeatedly harassed tenants. He'd told people that they would have to move out, offered buyouts, and demanded an elderly tenant sign papers that would end her tenancy while her grandson was away at work. KATC suggested tenants hold a meeting at the buildings. At the meeting, tenants agreed to form a group and refuse to move out. They made a plan to confront the landlord's agent with a letter signed by all tenants that would put him on notice that tenants were staying in their homes. Someone created a group chat for tenants to share information and let everyone know when they next see the landlord's agent at the buildings. Since the meeting, there has been no sign of the landlord's agent and no more harassment.

Because KATC members understand from their own experience that the sale of a building often portends displacement pressures, the group will reach out to tenants if they learn a building in the area is for sale. When a low-rise building across the street from 2419 Keele Street was for sale in 2024, flyers went under all the doors and someone responded right away. A meeting was held in the hallway of the main floor, with several tenants from 2419 Keele crossing the street to speak with their neighbours, joined by other KATC members. They warned the tenants that their landlord may try to push them out prior to a sale or that a new owner could also try. They described how they had organized against renoviction and urged their neighbours to do the same if it came to it. Tenants at the building now know that if their landlord attempts to push them out, they have the support of neighbours in the area.

When the crew from 2419 Keele crossed the street to speak with their neighbours about their own fight against renoviction, some tenants said they had heard about the struggle back in 2021. They had seen it on the news, or had seen the posters tenants put up along the street, or had received the newsletter tenants had distributed after their eviction notices had been withdrawn. The struggle had happened in their neighbourhood, had been waged by ordinary working-class people like them, living in an apartment building similar to theirs. In a moment when tenants were uncertain about what would happen as their building is sold, they could be certain that if their new landlord tried to push them out, then not only did they possess the capacity to fight back to keep their homes, but their neighbours across the street would be there alongside them.

District-based organizing in the Keele area has multiplied organizing against renovictions in aggregate and effectiveness. KATC members are tenants who distinguish themselves from other working-class people in the Keele area only by the experience they have gained organizing to stop renovictions and improve housing conditions and by their shared commitment to support others to do the same. Organizing with other working-class people in their district, KATC has contested the ability of landlords to evict tenants and begun to challenge the power of the state to enable displacement.

FOUR

Renoviction and the State

The apparent rise in renovictions and the attention they receive has led to calls for various levels of government to intervene and prevent the practice. Academics, housing advocates, and non-profits have identified state intervention as crucial for protecting tenants and our so-called "affordable housing stock."[1] In turn, different levels of government have proposed and introduced measures meant to stop renovictions.

In this chapter, we examine state responses to renoviction alongside state intervention in housing more generally to show how existing forms of administration have featured in cases of renoviction. We begin with a brief history of Canadian state intervention in the housing field since the Second World War, to help establish how class struggles over housing may change the form of the state. Next, we look at how various levels of government have responded to increased opposition to renoviction. Focusing on the renoviction bylaws recently adopted in Hamilton, Toronto, and elsewhere, we argue that these efforts channelled opposition to renoviction into political, legal, and bureaucratic channels, resulting in new forms of administration. We then discuss how the state furnishes landlords with the legal means to retaliate against organized tenants and how the state and landlords have attempted to undermine present-day tenant organizing. We conclude by looking at how the state neutralizes opposition to urban displacement.

HOUSING AND THE CANADIAN STATE

Historically, the federal, provincial, and municipal levels of the Canadian state have intervened in the housing field in response to class struggles—including struggles over evictions, rent increases, and housing conditions—that challenge the state's power to maintain the conditions for capital accumulation within its territory. The state has introduced housing reforms to contain working-class struggles for improved housing conditions and to prevent those struggles from overturning the conditions for rent extraction. Some housing reforms, such as implementing rent regulations or building government-owned public housing, may provisionally appease the public, stabilize the political-economic situation, and even improve conditions for some sections of the working class. Other housing reforms, such as ending public housing programs or prohibiting rent withholding, for example, clearly worsen conditions for renters and undermine working-class organizing. In any case, the state intervenes and changes its form to contain and redirect class struggles that challenge its power.

In 1941, the federal government incorporated Wartime Housing Limited (WHL) to administer its first rental housing program. From 1941 to 1946, WHL built twenty-five thousand rental units in response to the demands of the war effort and workers' struggles that arose from rapid industrialization and urbanization, such as the massive wartime strike wave of 1942–43.[2] During the war, increasing political pressure to meet the housing needs of evicted soldiers' families and the urban poor led WHL to make agreements with municipal governments to build public housing projects. However, before the war's end, the federal finance department curtailed WHL's activity to prevent the extensive socialization of housing, and by the early 1950s, WHL's housing stock was liquidated into the private house market.[3]

In the postwar period, political stability rested on the social and political integration of the working class based on the sustained domestic accumulation of capital to keep down the costs of social reform. The state sought to integrate the working class through a system of labour relations—including collective bargaining—that managed class conflict in the workplace, and through suburbanization and home ownership to relieve the pressures of rapid urbanization and disperse urban-based struggles. Sustained capital accumulation relied on a planned reconstruction effort based on the technological development of the means of production, including methods of high-rise apartment construction, and social reforms to meet the aspirations of the working class, such as the limited provision of public housing.[4] However, the state sought to ensure as much as possible that workers would access housing through the private market. In 1945, the Central Mortgage and Housing Corporation (CMHC) was created to shutter and privatize the wartime housing program and to finance and rationalize private, suburban house construction and individual home ownership. In the 1960s, to relieve the pressures of urbanization and the increasing militancy of Canadian workers in workplaces and cities, CMHC financed apartment construction. A small portion of apartments became government-owned public housing—public housing that was nonetheless built by private developers.[5]

The state-supported apartment boom of the 1960s and 1970s created highly profitable private housing developers and powerful government-owned public housing authorities that worked to subdue the growing strength of militant construction workers in Toronto, whose city-wide strikes threatened to disrupt crucial urban development projects such as apartment construction and subway expansion. Throughout those decades, corporate land developers acquired much of the vacant land in the urban fringes of Canadian cities. Vertical integration of these firms meant they had in-house units specializing in realty, engineering, construction, property management, and other functions required to develop vacant land. Horizontal integration allowed firms to operate across the commercial, residential, and industrial sectors and switch investment based on opportunity. In this period, the average annual rate of return on corporate apartment investment was 50.2 percent and high-rise apartments were especially profitable. By 1969, the cost of land in Toronto made up 50 percent of the cost of housing.

As land prices rose, high-rise apartments became more attractive to developers. While the per unit construction costs for an apartment were about the same as a standard suburban house, land for an apartment unit was one-sixth the price of a house.[6] Federal funding for public housing flowed to provincial housing corporations such as the Ontario Housing Corporation (OHC) and increased the demand for high-rise apartments. The apartment boom spurred technological development of construction methods. The increased application of building materials like concrete and drywall, and the introduction of new labour processes such as the "flying form" scaffolding method, deskilled workers, undermined craft unionism, and enabled profitable corporate developers to consolidate.[7] The OHC relied on these developers, preferring to purchase existing units and units already under construction rather than spend more on new public housing developments under government contracts with union wage rates.[8]

Expansionary US policies in the postwar period had stimulated capital accumulation on a world scale, providing the basis for the governments of core capitalist countries to expand welfare policies. However, accumulation in manufacturing began to run ahead of the supply of raw materials, especially oil, and the boom ended in 1974.[9] In Canada, as elsewhere, the rising costs of public housing subsidies and other social programs contributed to inflationary pressures and the fiscal crisis of the state. From 1973 to 1975, rents in the metropolitan Toronto area increased by 31 percent.[10] The class struggle intensified with a wave of wildcat strikes and a rise in tenant organizing, including high-profile rent strikes in Toronto. Tenants in Toronto's Regent Park public housing project organized against rising rents and demanded recreational facilities and greater control over property management.[11] Tenants in privately owned apartments at 33 Eastmount Avenue and 103–105 West Lodge Avenue went on rent strike against unacceptable housing conditions.[12] The OHC created a joint Tenant-OHC Management Board to co-opt the Regent Park tenants' organization, the courts drew the rent strikers into prolonged legal cases, and Ontario amended landlord-tenant law to prohibit rent withholding. In 1975, Ontario enacted rent review, limiting rent increases for most tenants to 8 percent unless a landlord could prove operating expense increases at a tribunal. Ontario also introduced the requirement for municipal authorization to evict tenants for demolition, conversion, and renovation.[13] The state thus contained the upsurge in tenant organizing and maintained the conditions for rent extraction.

A wave of plant closures in southern Ontario beginning in the 1970s and 1980s broke up the centralized production system there and weakened the working-class movement.[14] Federal government transfer payments for public and non-profit housing declined throughout the 1970s and 1980s as the state cut social programs. Lower levels of rental housing production and rent regulation led to a spike in evictions for demolition, renovation, and condominium conversions, as landlords found new ways to raise rent revenues.[15] In the mid-1990s, the union-led, extraparliamentary movement against neoliberal restructuring in Ontario split on the question of electoral support for the NDP and was unable to mount an effective opposition. The failure of the working class to overcome sectional divisions made it possible for the state to end the public housing program and deregulate rents.[16] In 1995, federal funding for public housing ended. Two years later, Ontario eliminated rent control on vacant units between tenants, instituting vacancy decontrol, and removed landlord-tenant cases from the provincial court system, creating an administrative tribunal to handle them.[17] Vacancy decontrol allowed for a rapid rise in average rents that more than made up for the estimated 15 percent rent depression attributable to the period of stronger rent regulation from 1976 to 1996.[18]

Knowing the history of Canadian state intervention in the housing field can help us understand the state's involvement in renoviction today. Upsurges in working-class struggle are transformed into new forms of administration that reproduce the working class as a class divorced from any independent way of supporting itself:

> Administration is working-class power *post festum*; working-class political victories captured and formalized at their moment of triumph . . . every innovation, new body, tribunal, or commission originates either directly or at one remove from working-class resistance to the formal conditions of its life.[19]

Currently, the state creates conditions that enable renoviction and, although the level of working-class organization and struggle is low, is sensitive to growing opposition to renoviction. Rather than protecting tenants from displacement, the state contains and redirects opposition to renoviction to maintain the conditions for rent extraction.

POLICY RESPONSES TO RENOVICTION

We can appreciate the transformation of working-class struggles against eviction into new forms of administration through the introduction of, and discussions surrounding, municipal renoviction policies in Toronto and other cities in Ontario. In 2019, the City of Toronto's Planning and Housing Committee created a subcommittee to look into the impact of renoviction on the supply of affordable rental housing and how the City could help tenants by preventing renovictions. Following high-profile cases like 795 College Street and what a City staff report called "growing public interest" in the issue, the Subcommittee on the Protection of Affordable Rental Housing convened in November 2019 and for three hours heard deputations from tenants who had experienced renoviction and from tenant advocates urging the City to take action.[20] At the end of the meeting, councillor Gord Perks noted, "Every once in a while here at city hall something happens—there's a meeting like this—where you get the sense that something big is about to change."

The subcommittee would meet a few more times over the next few years, creating advisory committees and work plans, and promising to explore ways to collect data on renovictions, which the City characterized as cases where tenants are evicted "illegitimately." A bylaw adopted by New Westminster, British Columbia, in 2019 to prevent renoviction was touted as an example for the City to study and follow. Tenants and their (self-appointed) representatives in the non-profit sector were incorporated into the policy-making process. Instead of organizing with neighbours to fight evictions, tenants attended meetings with City staff and prepared presentations. Some tenants who were drawn into the process were frustrated by what they took to be the City's lack of interest in taking meaningful action and had their participation limited to minor consultative or advisory roles.

While the subcommittee and the media coverage of various meetings and City reports gave the impression that something was being done at the municipal level to address the problem, many tenants across Toronto over these years focused on organizing at their buildings to fight back against renoviction and defend their homes. During this time, tenants living at 12 Lansdowne Avenue, 394 Dovercourt Road, 14 Wadsworth Boulevard, 2419 Keele Street, and 1570 Lawrence Avenue West, and in less high profile cases we are familiar with, beat renoviction by organizing with their neighbours.

Despite the City of Toronto's vast resources, it did not engage in any independent data collection or succeed in documenting the actual incidence of renovictions in Toronto. The main products of the City's subcommittee were a framework for a renoviction bylaw that sat on the shelf until 2024, an eviction prevention handbook for tenants, and an online tool for tenants that provided information about different apartment renovations. The latter two help illuminate how City staff and councillors understand renoviction, which in turn shapes the City's overall approach to the issue.

The City of Toronto's eviction prevention handbook, discussed in previous chapters, facilitates displacement. The handbook focuses on the legal eviction process and the rules a landlord must follow to "legitimately" evict a tenant. In its section on eviction for renovations and N13 notices, the handbook advises tenants: "Your landlord can evict you if they want to repair or renovate the building or unit" and "If you receive an N13, you are not required to move out and you have the right to an LTB hearing." The handbook then lists different types of renovations and the "likelihood of you needing to move out during the renovation."[21] By narrowly focusing on the legal eviction process and on the renovations proposed by a landlord, the handbook obscures the fact that renovictions are primarily about displacement. The handbook in fact does the same work performed by many landlord agents—it emphasizes the potential disruptions caused by the proposed renovation work and encourages tenants who insist on challenging the eviction to do so through the legal process. Such a document could only be produced by people who believe there are landlords who "legitimately" evict tenants in order to upgrade rental units and welcome those same tenants back, despite the complete lack of evidence for such a belief.

As if that were not enough, the handbook uncritically encourages tenants to assert their right of first refusal and even includes a template letter tenants can use to notify their landlord of their intention to move back into their unit after the renovations are completed. As far as we are aware, this is not something that happens following an eviction for extensive renovations on an N13 notice. While the City's handbook does not at all suggest that asserting a right of first refusal may in practice be difficult, it does let tenants know that they can file an application with the LTB if this right is violated—something that will not get a tenant back into their unit once a new tenant is brought in at higher rent.

The City's online Renovation Rights Assessment Tool expands on the list of renovations included in its handbook and provides feedback to tenants based on their individual responses to a questionnaire. After completing the questionnaire, a tenant who has received an N13 eviction notice will receive an assessment of whether or not they will need to move out and be told "You do not have to move out right away!" Ignoring how this information simply facilitates displacement and implies some tenants will have to move out at some point in the process, it is hard to imagine something more useless to tenants facing renoviction than this online tool. Landlords renovict tenants because they want to bring in new, higher-paying tenants, not because they are primarily motivated to conduct extensive in-unit renovation work. From the perspective of a tenant, a landlord's renovation plans are irrelevant, and tenants are best served by ignoring these details unless they are preparing for a hearing at the LTB. When a landlord says they want a tenant to move out so they can renovate, the key point is that the landlord is trying to push the tenant out. If the tenant deems this unacceptable, then they can and should fight back and motivate their landlord to change their plans. Renovictions are dynamic situations, and tenants have the ability to change their landlord's plans. Tenants are not powerless and do not need to submit to renoviction, even if their landlord is proposing extensive renovations that municipal staff have decided could require vacant possession to carry out.

In 2024, the City of Hamilton approved a renoviction bylaw. The move was celebrated by tenant advocates, with lawyer Karen Andrews of the Advocacy Centre for Tenants Ontario saying the bylaw would help fix "a terrible problem" and eliminate renoviction "scams" but still allow so-called "honest" landlords to carry out renovations as needed.[22] The bylaw requires landlords to apply for a renovation licence after they have issued N13 eviction notices to tenants. Landlords have to submit a building permit and a report from a "qualified person" that vacant possession is required for the renovations. However, obtaining a building permit is not difficult for landlords and many landlords already hire professionals who can provide reports to the City that vacant possession is needed.[23] Moreover, these measures do not really change the requirements for landlords to renovict tenants.

The key change introduced by the bylaw is the requirement that landlords provide temporary accommodations or rental top-up payments to evicted tenants who say they want to return to their apartments after the renovations are completed. This is similar to the City of Toronto's rules around demoviction, where the City intervenes to manage the displacement of tenants to some extent, working with developers to get tenants to sign agreements for compensation and replacement units in the new development.[24] Landlords seeking a renovation licence will have to show the City that they have come to an agreement with a tenant regarding temporary accommodations, or for "severance compensation" where a tenant agrees to permanently give up their apartment. If landlords are found to have violated the bylaw, they could face fines.

After Hamilton introduced their renoviction bylaw, Toronto adopted a similar bylaw in 2024, and other cities in Ontario have either introduced their own renoviction bylaws or are considering doing so.[25] In Toronto, tenant advocates celebrated the new Rental Renovation Licence Bylaw that the City says will "protect tenants and prevent renovictions" as well as "preserve Toronto's affordable rental housing and establish a transparent and equitable process for landlords to complete necessary renovations responsibly."[26] Mayor Olivia Chow proclaimed, "Those landlords that are using renovations as an excuse to evict people, you can't get away with it now."[27] However, the bylaws introduced in Hamilton and Toronto do not actually prohibit renoviction—they do not stop landlords from evicting tenants in order to conduct renovations and will instead increase the pressure on tenants to submit to renoviction.

As we have seen, even though tenants in Ontario have a formal right to return to their unit after renovations have been completed, once tenants move out, it is practically impossible to return. Landlords who renovict tenants instead bring in new, higher-paying tenants to occupy renovated units. If tenants move out, they lose control of their housing. Yet the bylaws encourage tenants to move out, with municipalities promising to protect tenants' interests afterwards.

Those advocating most strongly for these bylaws and celebrating their adoption typically misunderstand renoviction, ignore the capacity of working-class tenants to organize against renoviction, and overestimate the effectiveness of existing bylaws relating to rental housing.

Cities like Hamilton and Toronto have demonstrated an inability to enforce their property standards bylaws in renoviction cases. For example, tenants in one Hamilton building went without water for three months as their landlord tried to force them out.[28] The City initially ordered the landlord to fix the issue within a month. The landlord then appealed the order and the City gave the landlord many more weeks to fix it. Tenants in another Hamilton building where the landlord had issued N13 eviction notices went without heat for weeks, even after the City ordered the landlord to fix it.[29] Tenants at two Toronto buildings reported that even after the City ordered the landlords to do certain repairs, repairs would not be done and the landlords would continue to neglect the buildings.

Property standards staff often defer to landlords while dismissing tenant concerns. When Ottawa tenants fighting renoviction complained to the City about the lack of heat in their apartments, the City reached out to the landlord to ask if he would be responding to the heat complaint and whether the tenants would be vacating soon. After the landlord denied receiving a call about the heat issue and falsely claimed there was a plan to relocate the tenants, City staff simply thanked the landlord and said everything was good. When tenants at 1570 Lawrence Avenue West in Toronto called the City to complain about their landlord installing a pipe in their apartment so that tenants in other, newly renovated units could have in-unit laundry, City staff told them that they should be happy their landlord was upgrading the building. At another Toronto building where tenants were fighting evictions, harassment, disrepair, and a persistent lack of heating they had contacted the City about, the City inspector wrote to the landlord praising the work of the property manager and lamenting the tenants' poor conduct and said he would write to the tenants to remind them of the importance of working with building management.

We are also familiar with cases where municipal property standards and fire department staff have been even more directly involved in facilitating renoviction. At one Parkdale building, the landlord issued N13s to tenants in four units, claiming it was in order to comply with a City order to install a new sprinkler system, then had a district chief from the fire department testify at the LTB hearing in support of the eviction case.[30] At another LTB hearing, the tenants summoned a building inspector to give an opinion on how long the work described in the N13s would take to complete, only for the inspector to tell the LTB that while he was aware of cases where tenants continued to live in units while similar work was done, he could not say that would be possible in these tenants' case. Another building inspector ordered the landlord of a Keele area building to have an engineer inspect the building, then told tenants that it would be up to the landlord's contractor whether or not they would have to move out during repairs. This inspector blocked the phone number of one tenant at the building who tried to reach him to get more information. After another group of tenants resisted harassment and buyout offers at a Toronto rooming house, the landlord sought the opinion of a fire inspector, whose advice to the landlord was to evict the tenants and convert the building into a single-family home in order to avoid having to comply with municipal rooming house regulations.

Meanwhile, the City of Toronto's regulations around demoviction are not as effective as people assume. In practice, many tenants are pushed out of their homes by developers prior to being issued formal eviction notices and signing agreements for replacement units and interim compensation. There is also hardly any oversight of these agreements, and many tenants do not end up moving back into replacement units following demolition and construction. When tenants do move back in, some find that the units are not as promised, or that they are treated differently by the developer compared to those who are not moving into replacement units. In practice, landlords and developers flout these regulations. Nearly twenty years after the regulations were introduced, tenants continue to voice concerns about demoviction; however, many tenants now focus on lobbying the City for better compensation packages rather than resisting eviction at their buildings.[31]

Hamilton's and Toronto's renoviction bylaws can be

understood as a state response to working-class organizing that adds a layer of municipal administration to the legal eviction process for extensive renovations that landlords are expected to follow. The bylaws give the impression that steps are being taken to stop renoviction, without actually prohibiting eviction for extensive renovation via the LTB or preventing landlords from using informal approaches and extralegal tactics to push tenants out of their homes. The bylaws also reinforce the mistaken ideas that there are landlords issuing N13 eviction notices because they simply want to upgrade rental properties for existing tenants, and that if tenants know their rights then they will not be displaced. It is only if one mistakenly believes that renovictions are cases where tenants are evicted "illegally" or "illegitimately" because landlords break certain rules or do not actually conduct extensive renovations that one can have the mistaken impression that if no laws are violated then tenants will not be displaced. Municipal governments are also aware that the precondition for increasing their property tax revenues—raising rents and land values—often involves displacing tenants. The local state thus obscures the issue to confuse would-be opponents of renoviction so that landlords may proceed with closing rent gaps unchallenged.

What the bylaws passed in Hamilton and Toronto promise to do is increase the pressure on tenants to submit to eviction if their landlord produces paperwork that the state deems acceptable. Tenants are now up against not only their landlord and potentially the LTB, but the City as well. By trying to force landlords to compensate evicted tenants more than they are currently required to under provincial law, the state relies on the social power of money to facilitate displacement and undermine tenant organizing.[32] As scholars Geoffrey Kay and James

Mott write, "Every movement of the working class that threatens to breach procedure has been countered with administrative initiatives . . . not only to contain struggles-in-process, but to minimize opposition."[33] Municipal governments have dedicated considerable resources toward transforming working-class struggles against renoviction into new forms of administration over the process of urban displacement. Municipal administration of the eviction process risks doing more to legitimize eviction for extensive renovations and undermine tenant organizing than it will prevent displacement. Tenants may receive higher buyout offers from landlords, but landlords will continue to have a financial incentive to push out sitting tenants and raise rents on vacant units.

Policy responses to renoviction in other jurisdictions over the past few years similarly do not stop landlords from displacing tenants or address extralegal tactics used by landlords to push out existing tenants in order to conduct renovations.

Since 2018, Doug Ford's government in Ontario has weakened protections for renters, limiting tenants' ability to raise issues at non-payment of rent eviction hearings and eliminating rent control on newly constructed rental units. The government has also twice increased the maximum fines allowable for landlords found to have evicted tenants in bad faith and introduced other measures that do not fundamentally change the existing requirements on landlords for evicting tenants for extensive renovations.[34]

However, increasing fines does not deter landlords from renovicting tenants. For one, it is exceedingly rare for the LTB to find that a landlord has evicted a tenant in bad faith and issue a fine. This is because the onus is on the evicted tenant to file an application against the landlord at the LTB and prove their case at a hearing. As we have seen, well-resourced landlords have a distinct advantage at the LTB over working-class tenants, who generally lack the time and money needed to bring a legal case forward, let alone hire a lawyer or paralegal to represent them. Second, even if the LTB fines a landlord, the landlord can quickly recoup that money through the higher rents they charge on vacated units and, possibly, profit on the sale of the building.

Recall that in the case of 795 College Street, the LTB fined Evan Johnsen and Neil Spiegel $75,000, only for them to renovict tenants at 12 Lansdowne Avenue a few years later, despite the maximum fines being raised in the intervening years. Because renoviction is potentially so profitable, increasing fines has not deterred landlords from renovicting tenants—something worth keeping in mind in the context of the municipal bylaws discussed above.

In Nova Scotia, the government responded to growing public concern over renoviction since the COVID-19 pandemic with new measures in 2022 requiring landlords to obtain a permit to evict tenants for extensive renovations, similar to the rules in Ontario. These measures gave the public the impression that, amid a growing eviction crisis in the province, the government was doing something to curb renoviction. However, fixed-term leases, which do not automatically renew and therefore undermine tenants' security of tenure, remain legal in the province. In response to the new rules surrounding eviction for extensive renovations, Nova Scotia landlords have increasingly signed tenants to fixed-term leases. This way, landlords can avoid the scrutiny they might receive for renovicting tenants by simply refusing to renew tenants' leases. Fixed-term leases have now become so integral to landlords closing rent gaps in rental housing units in Halifax that real estate sales listings for rental buildings highlight the presence of tenants on fixed-term leases at buildings to attract prospective buyers.[35]

In 2021, Prince Edward Island banned eviction for renovations for two years, except when the renovations were necessary "to protect or preserve the property" or its residents and when a building permit was obtained.[36] Before the moratorium ended, new legislation was passed that now requires landlords to provide tenants with several months' notice before evicting them for renovations and giving tenants the formal right to return after the renovations are done.[37]

More recently, the Government of Quebec put in place a three-year moratorium on eviction for dividing or enlarging apartments. The moratorium on certain types of eviction came a few months after the government had passed a controversial law making it easier for landlords to refuse a tenant transferring their lease—tenants protesting that law said it would lead to higher rents, as lease transfers are a mechanism for tenants to keep rents down.[38] The moratorium on evicting tenants in order to divide or enlarge apartments could be in place for less than three years in cities where the vacancy rate reaches 3 percent.[39] More importantly, the temporary ban on certain types of eviction does not prevent landlords' extralegal renoviction tactics or address other approaches used by landlords to renovict tenants.[40]

RETALIATION AGAINST TENANT ORGANIZING

The state not only creates the conditions that make renoviction possible and profitable, it also furnishes landlords with the legal means to retaliate against organized tenants. When tenants refuse to submit to the administration of eviction, landlords and the state counter with new threats of eviction, financial penalties, and other legal threats. In the class struggle, the state extends its legal, administrative, and bureaucratic forms to repress, contain, and divert working-class organizing against rent extraction. Neither a neutral arbiter nor an open, institutional terrain of contestation between landlords and tenants, the capitalist state is instead the political form of a class-antagonistic society in which rent organizes, and immiserates, urban life.[41]

Landlords have characterized tenant organizing as illegal, or even violent, criminal activity. In March 2022, landlords Evan Johnsen and Neil Spiegel issued eviction notices to tenants at 12 Lansdowne Avenue alleging that hanging banners from their balconies naming the landlords and calling on them to stop the evictions constituted "substantial interference" (i.e., N5) and "illegal activity" (i.e., N6) under the *Residential Tenancies Act*. Later that month, a detective from the Toronto Police Service (TPS) knocked on doors at 12 Lansdowne. The detective told tenants he was leading a criminal investigation into posters distributed throughout the Parkdale neighbourhood, posters that named their landlords, Evan Johnsen and Neil Spiegel, and called on them to drop the renovictions. In another case, TPS visited tenants from 2841 Keele Street after they protested renoviction at their landlord's home. In both cases, tenants refused police interviews and no charges were laid.

After tenants at 2419 Keele Street succeeded in getting landlord Brendan Riley to withdraw the N13 eviction notices issued to them, Riley filed peace bond applications against tenants in provincial court alleging tenants threatened to personally injure him or damage his property. Although tenants we spoke with said Riley eventually withdrew the applications, tenants had to secure legal representation for multiple court appearances. More recently, in an apparent attempt to use the media to criminalize tenant organizing, landlord Lankin Investments said a noisy protest at its head office organized by tenants from 1570 Lawrence Avenue West resulted in "violence, physical injury and assault of our staff and security."[42]

When tenants have prevented their landlord from harassing them with in-unit inspections or have protested outside their landlord's home, landlords have submitted complaints to Ontario's Rental Housing Enforcement Unit (RHEU). Tenants challenging renoviction at one building received letters from RHEU threatening $50,000 fines after tenants collectively refused the landlord entry to their units due to the landlord's repeated unit inspections that they considered harassment. After tenants from 1570 Lawrence Avenue West protested renovictions outside the home of landlord Kyle Pulis, RHEU called to inform us that the landlord wanted us investigated for committing offences under the *Residential Tenancies Act* despite us not residing at the landlord's building. In neither of these cases were tenants fined or evicted for the alleged offences.

Landlords have issued and threatened to issue formal eviction notices against tenant organizers, alleging their participation in organizing amounted to "substantial interference" and "illegal activity." Tenants from 1570 Lawrence Avenue West received lawyer's letters threatening $50,000 fines and eviction for "Wrongful Conduct" after they protested outside Kyle Pulis's home. Lankin Investments never followed up on these threats. Parkdale tenants from 12 Lansdowne Avenue defeated their landlords' attempts to criminalize their organizing by refusing to back down in the face of eviction notices for hanging banners from their balconies in protest of renoviction. In March 2021, hundreds of tenants from Toronto's Parkdale neighbourhood marched through the district in defence of organizers at 55 Triller Avenue who were organizing against poor conditions at their building. Landlord Starlight Investments had targeted three organizers at the building with eviction for the alleged "illegal act" of collectively delivering a demand letter to the property management office, but withdrew the evictions in the face of pressure from tenants in the neighbourhood.[43] Landlords' frequent legal action against tenant organizers nonetheless indicates the potential for the state to turn its legal and administrative power against working-class organizers.

In a number of cases, landlords have also threatened to file civil lawsuits against tenants fighting renoviction. Tenants in Toronto have received cease and desist letters from lawyers demanding they remove news articles and social media posts, alleging flyers distributed in the area of their landlord's office were libellous, and insisting they stop warning prospective tenants about the landlord and conditions at the building during viewings of vacant, renovated units.

Housing researcher Andrew Crosby documents how Timbercreek Asset Management, now Hazelview Properties, made legal threats against the Herongate Tenant Coalition (HTC). Timbercreek's threats were meant to suppress HTC's organizing in opposition to the mass evictions the landlord carried out against tenants from the Heron Gate neighbourhood in south Ottawa. Through public meetings, demonstrations, and a social media campaign, HTC so thoroughly exposed Timbercreek for evicting hundreds of disproportionately racialized tenants in Heron Gate that Timbercreek rebranded as Hazelview in 2020. In retaliation, Timbercreek sent HTC a series of cease and desist letters, called the police on tenants protesting outside the Timbercreek office in Heron Gate, and wrote to Twitter demanding HTC's account be permanently disabled. In its letter to Twitter, Timbercreek described HTC members as "unstable," "unhinged," and "extremist." As Crosby writes, "the threat of sanction under civil law [is] a creative form of repression within liberal democracies" that Timbercreek used aggressively against HTC.[44]

Recently, the state has also shown a willingness to exercise its administrative power in unprecedented directions to undermine tenant organizing. In May 2023, over one hundred tenants living at 71, 75, and 79 Thorncliffe Park Drive in Toronto began withholding rent in protest of above guideline rent increases sought by landlords PSP Investments and Starlight Investments.[45] In addition to withholding rent, tenants protested the rent increases at their landlord's offices, at the homes of executives and board members, and at events where the landlords were present. After the landlords submitted a request to fast-track the above guideline rent increase hearings—citing the tenants' organizing efforts and withholding of rent, though mischaracterizing tenant protests as unlawful and even violent activity—the LTB issued an unprecedented order to shorten the time to the hearings.[46] The LTB granted the landlords' request without a hearing, denying tenants the ability to respond to the landlords' submissions. In light of this LTB decision, landlords whose tenants resist renoviction may try to fast-track the eviction process in the same manner.

NON-RELIANCE ON THE STATE

The class struggle touches every aspect of housing: from struggles at the point of housing production on construction sites and factory floors, to land-based Indigenous-led struggles, to struggles for welfare benefits and public housing, to migrant farmworker struggles against unacceptable housing conditions, to tenants' building- and district-based struggles against renoviction. Although maintaining the labour force requires the majority of workers to have access to housing, the purpose of capitalist housing production is not to meet the social need for housing but to appropriate profit and accumulate capital. Tenants experience exploitation both economically and politically: the state enforces rent payment with eviction. When tenants organize, they not only undermine the landlord's sources of revenue, they also challenge the rights of private property. In the class struggle, the state intervenes to contain workers' struggles within new forms of administration, precipitating changes in the form of the state. The state cannot resolve the contradiction at the heart of capitalist housing production; it can only complement the power of capital in class struggles over housing.[47]

Yet the protective role of the state in housing its citizens looms large in current debates around housing. The state can counteract the inability of the market to meet the social need for housing by funding public housing and curb the excesses of landlords by administering the landlord-tenant relationship. Many on the left call on the state to enact policies they argue will not only improve the condition of less fortunate citizens, but reduce the mounting costs that precarious housing and related social ills impose on society.

When it comes to contemporary discussions of housing from the perspective of tenants, a social democratic approach is prevalent. Tenant partisans lament how governments have failed renters while remaining optimistic about state power. In *The Tenant Class*, Ricardo Tranjan writes that the state can rebalance tenants' power and status in relation to other social groups through increased rental market regulation and housing provisioning.[48] Despite the state's repressive power, Tracy Rosenthal and Leonardo Vilchis want to abolish rent without being "state-phobic."[49] Nick Bano proposes the state should monopolize the rental housing sector, squeezing private landlords out altogether.[50] Each author makes a welcome contribution to a growing literature that underlines the importance of tenant organizing to urban class struggle. However, we question the authors' shared contention that tenants should aim to increase their influence within the state.

This chapter has argued that the social democratic approach to the state is inadequate for understanding how the state responds to class struggles over housing. Historically, the Canadian state has accommodated its interventions in the housing field to the imperative of rent extraction. At the highpoint of state intervention in the housing field in the 1960s and 1970s, the state implemented public housing programs and rent regulations that either helped create or did not suspend the conditions for capital accumulation within the state's territory. In the current period, in the face of growing opposition to renoviction in Ontario, the state invited tenants and tenant advocates into the policy-making process and developed new forms of administration that will safeguard the legal process of eviction for extensive renovation from challenges from self-organized tenants. These new administrative forms are layered on top of existing forms that already enable landlords to retaliate against organized tenants with threats of eviction, financial penalties, criminal charges, and fast-tracked rent increases. Non-profits and tenant advocates have been enthusiastic about cooperating with the state to develop and promote these new forms of administration that give them access to more funding and increase their profiles, allowing them to reproduce and enlarge their organizations. By undertaking a class analysis of the state, it is possible to appreciate how the state incorporates and undermines class struggles over housing.

Reformist initiatives that focus on policy solutions and state intervention occupy the political space working-class people need for independent organizing strategies to generalize. Over the past several years, momentum tenants built organizing against renoviction has been redirected toward lobbying politicians. Non-profits have played a prominent role in redirecting this energy into initiatives that they can then profit from, in the form of expanded municipal funding and grant money to advise and inform tenants about new policies and help tenants navigate new bureaucracies of displacement and legal avenues. For example, the non-profit ACORN played a prominent role in lobbying Hamilton and other cities to adopt a renoviction bylaw and is also a partner that helps administer Hamilton's Tenant Support Program to help tenants facing renoviction and other issues. A tenant lawyer we interviewed said ACORN has also held meetings with legal clinic housing lawyers from cities across Ontario to strategize about how to redirect tenant opposition to renoviction into legal cases at the LTB against landlords who use the renoviction strategy. Advocates and non-profits work with the state to prevent the spread of public discourses on the potential power of self-organized tenants who confront landlords and refuse to abide by the legal eviction process. The threat posed by working-class self-organization to landlords and the state is erased.

The state facilitates and administers renoviction because urban displacement is integral to rent extraction in the capitalist city. The legal, administrative, and bureaucratic forms surrounding renoviction develop in response to class struggles over housing that challenge landlords' and the state's authority to extract rent. The state develops these forms to reimpose the rent relation on the working class, even as it enshrines new rights and regulations for tenants and landlords.

In chapter 3, we argued that independent working-class organizing based in renter districts has the greatest potential to stop renovictions and to challenge the power of landlords and the state. On their own, the tenant organizing examples we present do not address the scale of the renoviction problem, let alone the broader housing question. Assessing the limited achievements of recent organizing against renoviction, some may conclude that only the state can solve the problem and direct their energies towards reformist initiatives. We think this is a mistake. The process of bringing housing under collective, working-class control can only emerge from independent working-class organizing because capital accumulation and rent extraction are the very premises of the capitalist state. The successful, albeit modest, examples of tenant organizing against renoviction we document represent only the nascent movements in a socialization process. More fully developed district-based organizing initiatives, however, could aim to negate eviction enforcement in their areas altogether, blockading sheriffs and police deployed to remove tenants from their homes. Generalizing the practice of eviction blockades would make it more difficult for the authorities to enforce evictions, and soon, landlords would have trouble collecting rent. History tells us that the state implements reforms like rent controls, vacancy control, eviction bans, and social housing programs in an effort to contain working-class organizing and the attendant process of socialization it has lost the capacity to control, not in response to the demands of advocates or coalitions of non-profits.

CONCLUSION

As rents across Canada continued to rise dramatically throughout the start of the 2020s and both the media and politicians focused their attention on housing issues, "renoviction" became—if it was not already—a catchall term used to denote what many perceived as the most predatory landlord practices, as distinct from the more mundane ways landlords exploit tenants, which are seen as palatable. In providing a relatively narrow definition of "renoviction," we seek to characterize a particular phenomenon taking place in cities across the country and capture a distinct landlord practice, one replicated most often by certain types of landlords, in certain types of buildings, and with a specific set of tactics.

We have shown that renoviction is a landlord strategy to permanently displace tenants from their homes by claiming they will renovate units. As a method of increasing landlords' rent revenues on a per unit basis, renoviction relies on specific economic conditions, including the presence of rent gaps. Renoviction is far from the only strategy used by landlords to displace tenants and close rent gaps. However, while sharing certain features with, or being similar in certain respects to, other strategies—like eviction for personal use, demoviction, and above guideline rent increases—renoviction is a distinct landlord strategy for pushing out long-term tenants.

Renoviction is not about landlords repairing aging, inadequately maintained apartment buildings in order to improve the quality of rental housing. Tenants are not being displaced as some by-product of their landlord's simple desire to renovate units to create open-concept apartments, turn one-bedroom apartments into two-bedroom units, or install in-suite laundry or upgraded plumbing, electrical, or HVAC systems. Displacing tenants, not renovation, is the primary objective. This is true even when landlords do complete the extensive renovations they say they want to do. If landlords were sincerely interested in improving the housing conditions of existing tenants, they would work with tenants to repair and upgrade tenants' homes without evicting them.

We have described in detail how landlords who renovict tenants draw from a playbook of legal and extra-legal tactics. Renoviction is sanctioned and enforced by the legal frameworks governing residential tenancies across the country. But besides using legal processes to evict tenants for extensive renovation, landlords push tenants out via informal approaches, neglecting repairs, harassing tenants, making it impossible for tenants to comfortably remain in their homes, as well as other forms of eviction and legal threats.

We also showed how the success of a landlord's renoviction strategy is far from a foregone conclusion. Tenants have exerted considerable influence on their landlords' plans. When tenants refuse to move out, they immediately begin to alter the way that renoviction plays out. When tenants organize and take collective action, they have beat renoviction altogether and kept their homes. Although examples of successful organizing against renoviction may not be as numerous as we would hope, the cases we have highlighted are instructive. The basic principles present in the organizing work of tenants we interviewed—self-organization, direct confrontation with landlords, and non-reliance on legal strategies—are straightforward and replicable, and have actually contested the power of landlords, in some cases disciplining landlords and altering their approaches at other buildings in the future.

At the same time, the relatively low level of independent organizing against renoviction—and of independent tenant organizing more generally—has made it easier for the state to direct increased opposition to renovictions into political, legal, and bureaucratic channels. Non-profits have assisted the state in bottling up opposition to renovictions by perpetuating the idea that the law protects tenants from "illegitimate" evictions.

As noted at the outset, poor data regarding renovictions makes it difficult to discuss the course of the practice over time. It's safe to say that renovictions were on the rise in the late 2010s and early 2020s, though this observation is based on flawed official records, anecdotal evidence, an apparent increase in the number of cases where tenants organized to challenge renoviction, and increased media coverage, including of struggles at particular buildings. Developments over the past few years may already be influencing this trend. Interest rates rose significantly in 2022 and 2023 and remain higher than even pre-pandemic levels, making it harder for firms to buy up apartment buildings and execute costly renovation programs.[1] Tenants organizing to fight back against renoviction disciplined particular landlords and may have had a broader impact in discouraging landlords from deploying the strategy. For example, Brendan Riley shuttered Riley Real Estate Ventures. And we are aware of a number of other landlords who stopped renovicting tenants or have become less aggressive in doing so after seeing their renoviction attempts defeated by organized tenants at one of their buildings. As renoviction got more public and media attention, it's also possible that certain landlords who would otherwise have engaged in the practice have shied away from it due to the potential costs. Because the quantitative data around renovictions is poor and many renovictions are informal, it may be difficult to say how exactly things are trending in the future.

While it is too early for us to assess how the new renoviction bylaws in Hamilton, Toronto, and elsewhere will administer renovictions in practice, we know that existing policies channel tenant grievances into the state and serve to delegitimize tenant organizing. In Ontario, the *Residential Tenancies Act* says that tenants evicted for extensive renovation may file a complaint with the Landlord and Tenant Board up to two years after they vacated the unit, if their landlord prevented them from exercising their right of return. However, if the LTB finds the landlord evicted the tenant in "bad faith" and rerented the unit, the only remedies are for landlords to pay financial compensation to the tenant and/or fines to the LTB. Fines do not deter landlords from renovicting tenants, because landlords recoup their losses by rerenting units at increased rents, and the LTB will not reinstate the tenancy of a renovicted tenant once the unit is rerented. The Ontario *Residential Tenancies Act* therefore provides a semblance of recourse to renovicted tenants while making renoviction possible and profitable for landlords—yet, politicians, non-profits, and the media uphold the LTB as the proper venue for renovicted tenants to contest renoviction, encouraging tenants to wait to "challenge" their renoviction at their LTB hearing and, if that fails, file a complaint after they have been permanently displaced. These same groups treat tenants who organize against eviction outside the LTB with skepticism and condescension, if not outright hostility and retaliatory action.

Tenants facing renoviction who move out with the belief that the City will protect them have no more recourse to get back into their home once they are evicted than tenants had prior to the introduction of these bylaws.

We believe that tenant organizing remains the most powerful countervailing force against renoviction. Despite rents for vacant units levelling off in some cities in late 2024, there is still a lot of money to be made if landlords can displace long-term tenants and rerent their homes to new tenants.[2] Ads for apartment buildings that are for sale continue to advertise "rental upside" and rent gaps. In these conditions, tenants can be sure that there will be landlords seeking to push them out of their homes, and also that they can challenge these attempts by organizing.

Recently, after one group of tenants in Hamilton discovered their building was for sale, they formed a committee and over the next few months they hatched an extraordinary plan: tenants demanded the landlord sell the building to a housing co-operative they would form or they would go public and confront prospective buyers to dissuade them. Remarkably, the landlord conceded to their demand and tenants were able to access low-interest financing to purchase the building and run it as a housing co-op. Although purchasing their building is not an option for most tenants facing renoviction and is not a strategy that can be replicated on a large scale, this case nonetheless demonstrates the resourcefulness of organized tenants.[3]

Organizing is a dynamic process in which working-class people develop their collective capacities. As such, there is likely no single organizing model tenants should rely on. The principles and tactics discussed here have been effective against renoviction and also against other strategies landlords use to displace tenants and close rent gaps, including eviction for own use and above guideline rent increases. It will be for working-class people to discover and demonstrate how such principles may be applied by greater numbers of tenants and at larger scales.

We should commend tenants who organize against renoviction at their buildings and in their renter districts. The accomplishments of tenants who beat renoviction by confronting their landlords are worthy of our admiration. However, beating renoviction by no means resolves every question related to the conditions of tenants' housing. Tenants who beat their landlord's first attempt to renovict them may well be faced by a second renoviction. Defeated landlords may decide to sell the building, and a new owner may be even more determined and committed to renoviction. And even when tenants do get a reprieve from renoviction, they may still contend with high rents, poor housing conditions, and unresponsive landlords. These conditions will continue to be reproduced for as long as the provision of housing needs is subordinated to rent, profit, and private property.

NOTES

INTRODUCTION

1 Jane Armstrong, "Joining Forces in the Face of 'Renoviction,'" *Globe and Mail* (Toronto), November 11, 2008.

2 For example, Amanda Stephenson, "How to Protect Yourself Against 'Renoviction' as Rental Markets Heat Up," *Canadian Press*, December 22, 2022; Melissa Mancini and David Common, "'Renoviction' Rates Soar Due to Big City Housing Crunch," *CBC News*, December 30, 2019; Emily Mathieu, "Tenants Say 'Flimsy' Law Opens Door to 'Renovictions,'" *Toronto Star*, March 23, 2018.

3 Matt Lundy, "Eviction Applications Spike in Ontario as Rents Soar, Vacancies Dwindle," *Globe and Mail* (Toronto), February 27, 2023; Stephenson, "How to Protect Yourself Against 'Renoviction.'"

4 Affordable Housing Challenge Project, *Advancing the Right to Housing in Toronto: Critical Perspectives on the GTA's Housing Crisis and How to Solve It* (Toronto: University of Toronto, 2022).

5 Justin Chandler, "Where the Parties Stand: On Rent Control," *TVO*, May 20, 2022; Rachelle Younglai, "Millions of Canadians Rent, but They Have Been Left Out of Federal Campaign Promises," *Globe and Mail* (Toronto), September 17, 2021; Clara Pasieka and Lucas Powers, "How Do Toronto's Mayoral Candidates Compare on Election Issues?," *CBC News*, June 14, 2023; Samantha Beattie,

"Hamilton to Become 1st Ontario City with Bylaw to Stop 'Bad Faith' Renovictions," *CBC News*, January 18, 2024.

6 Samantha Beattie, "1st-of-Its-Kind Anti-Renoviction Bylaw Taking Shape in Hamilton, as City Looks to Keep Tenants Housed," *CBC News*, August 18, 2023.

7 This book is based on our 2023 report on renovictions in Toronto. Chapters 1 and 2 hew most closely to the report, though they have been expanded and updated to include information from other jurisdictions and renoviction cases elsewhere in Canada. Chapter 3 expands on the discussion of organizing from the report, including the addition of the section on district-based organizing. Chapter 4 was added, expanding on the discussion of Toronto's first proposed renoviction bylaw from the report and its now-enacted bylaw in "Bylaws Won't Defeat Bad Landlords: Only Tenant Organizing Can," *Ricochet*, December 16, 2024, as well as expanding on our chapter on renovictions and the state in Violaine Jolivet and Catherine Cliche, *Logement: Crises Partout, Justice Nulle Part!* (Presses Universitaires de Laval, forthcoming). In preparing this book, we conducted interviews with organizers outside of Toronto, and reviewed literature and media coverage of renoviction cases across the country, as well as recent policies enacted relating to renovictions.

ONE: UNDERSTANDING RENOVICTION

1 City of Toronto, "Promoting the Security of Residential Rental Tenancies," November 5, 2019, toronto.ca.

2 City of Toronto, "Actions to Address Renovictions in Toronto," May 31, 2021, toronto.ca.

3 City of Toronto, "Renoviction Policy: Creating a Framework to Protect Affordable and Mid-Range Rental Homes and Deter Renovictions," City Council, July 19, 2022, PH35.18, toronto.ca.

4 Alliance to End Homelessness Ottawa, endhomelessnessottawa.ca.

5 Canadian Centre for Housing Rights and National Right to Housing Network, *Implementing the Right to Housing in Canada: Renovations and Upgrading* (2022), 7.

6 Advocacy Centre for Tenants Ontario, *We Can't Wait: Preserving Our Affordable Rental Housing in Ontario* (2019). The report relies on the number of L2 applications landlords filed on N13 notices with the LTB. Only in a small number of renoviction cases do landlords file L2 applications with the LTB.

7 Matt Lundy, "Eviction Applications Spike in Ontario as Rents Soar, Vacancies Dwindle," *Globe and Mail* (Toronto), February 27, 2023.

8 Faryal Diwan, William Turman, Drew Baird, Neelu Mehta, Aleksandra Petrovic, and Brian Doucet, *Mapping Displacement in Kitchener-Waterloo: Report* (2021).

9 City of Toronto, "Renoviction Policy: Creating a Framework to Protect Affordable and Mid-Range Rental Homes and Deter Renovictions"; Melissa Mancini and David Common, "'Renoviction' Rates Soar Due to Big City Housing Crunch," *CBC News*, December 30, 2019.

10 Julia Woodhall-Melnik, Tobin LeBlanc Haley, and Chloe Reiser, "Renovate to Evict: An Analysis of Media Discussions of Renoviction," *Housing Studies* (2025): 1 30.

11 Government of Ontario, *Residential Tenancies Act* (2006), Section 50.

12 Neil Smith, *Uneven Development: Nature, Capital, and the Production of Space* (Oxford: Basil Blackwell, 1984), 150. When we refer to the "higher" use of land, we mean uses that raise the economic value of land.

13 The Narwhal, "Trending Topic: Ontario's Greenbelt," *The Narwhal*, accessed October 30, 2025, thenarwhal.ca.

14 Rahul Gupta, "Irreplaceable: Housing Researchers Warn

of Bill 23 Impacts on Toronto's Existing Affordable Rental Inventory," *Novae Res Urbis*, December 2, 2022.

15 Canadian Centre for Housing Rights, "Rent Regulation Policies Across Canada," February 10, 2025.

16 Holly Cabrera, "Quebec Has Rent Control: So Why Are Apartment Prices Still Soaring?," *CBC News*, July 8, 2025.

17 Chris Fox, "Looking to Rent One-Bedroom Apartment in Toronto?: New Report Suggests You'll Pay More Than $2,500 a Month," *CTV News*, March 14, 2023; Rentals.ca and Urbanation, "July 2025 Rent Report."

18 Martine August and Alan Walks, "Gentrification, Suburban Decline, and the Financialization of Multi-Family Rental Housing: The Case of Toronto," *Geoform* (2018): 124–36; Martine August, "The Financialization of Canadian Multi-Family Rental Housing: From Trailer to Tower," *Journal of Urban Affairs* (2020): 975–97.

19 Lundy, "Eviction Applications Spike in Ontario."

20 Gabe Oatley, "Tribunal Rules Longtime Tenant Can Stay in Her Home, Dismissing Landlord's Personal-Use Eviction Attempt," *TorontoToday*, February 11, 2025.

21 Philip Zigman and Martine August, *Above Guideline Rent Increases in the Age of Financialization* (RenovictionsTO, 2021).

22 RREV is no longer in operation and is therefore no longer marketing itself to potential investors. The website is no longer active and Brendan Riley's LinkedIn profile lists his time as Founder and CEO of the firm as ending in 2022.

23 Lankin Investments, "Common Sense Real Estate Investing," 2022, 3. Available at sedar.com. In 2023, amid the ongoing and much-publicized fight against renoviction by tenants at 1570 Lawrence Avenue West, Pulis Investments rebranded as Lankin Investments. While the company name changed, they continued to operate the same funds and corporate entities. Meanwhile, regulatory documents (e.g. on sedar.com) that

had been listed under Pulis Investments' profile were moved to Lankin Investments' profile, though older documents continue to bear the older name and branding. We will use the company's new name throughout.

24 Victoria Gibson, "Renters Facing Eviction Found a Memo from Their New Landlord Saying They Wanted a New 'Demographic' of Tenant: The Company Says It Was a Mistake," *Toronto Star*, July 29, 2022.

25 Pulis Real Estate Trust and Pulis Real Estate LP2, "Offering Memorandum," May 13, 2022. Available at sedar.com. The corporate structure of Pulis Real Estate Trust and Pulis Real Estate LP 2 is complex (see p. 19 of memo). When people invest in the trust, they provide the "Partnership" with funds to acquire properties. We will use "Partnership" when quoting from the memo, but otherwise we will simply use "Lankin Investments."

26 Pulis Real Estate Trust and Pulis Real Estate LP2, "Offering Memorandum," 32.

27 Pulis Real Estate Trust and Pulis Real Estate LP2, "Offering Memorandum," 29.

28 Teviah Moro, "Renting to a 'Different Demographic' in Hamilton," *Spectator* (Hamilton), January 16, 2018; CBC News, "Tenants of North York Building Demand Landlord Rescind Eviction Notices," August 7, 2022; Nick Westoll, "Toronto Apartment Renovations Move Out Notices Spark Renewed Calls to Protect Tenants," *CityNews*, July 11, 2022; Jessica Durling, "'They're Making Our Lives Hell': Residents Accuse Powerful Brampton Landlord of Uprooting Families for Profit," *The Pointer*, September 7, 2022; Gibson, "Renters Facing Eviction Found a Memo."

29 Previously viewable by the public, this video is now private. Pinnacle Wealth Brokers, "Pinnacle Presents Pulis Real Estate Trust: Hear from Kyle Pulis and Jason Thomsen," 2021, youtube.com.

30 Moro, "Renting to a 'Different Demographic' in Hamilton."

31 Shauna Hunt and Jessica Bruno, "Keele Street Tenants Face Renoviction for Second Time," *CityNews*, September 24, 2021.

32 Philip Zigman and Cole Webber, "Only Working Class Organizing Can Defeat Renovictions," *The Maple*, December 8, 2021.

33 RREV is no longer in operation, see note 22. Riley Real Estate Ventures, "F.A.Q. Investor Q&A," archive.org.

34 Shane Dingman, "Toronto City Councillor Warns of Eviction Notices Issued During Pandemic," *Globe and Mail* (Toronto), May 6, 2020.

35 Riley Real Estate Ventures, facebook.com.

36 Riley Real Estate Ventures, "Lenders' Standpoint," 2020, youtube.com.

37 Addy, "About," addyinvest.ca.

38 Addy, "Addy (2 Wingreen Court) Corp Offering Memorandum," March 5, 2021, amazonaws.com.

39 Addy, "Addy (1476 Avenue Rd) Corp Offering Memorandum," November 6, 2020, amazonaws.com.

40 Woodhall-Melnik, LeBlanc Haley, and Reiser, "Renovate to Evict."

41 *Residential Tenancies Act*, Section 50: "A landlord may give notice of termination of a tenancy if the landlord requires possession of the rental unit in order to . . . (c) do repairs or renovations to it that are so extensive that they require a building permit and vacant possession of the rental unit."

42 Ontario Legislative Assembly, *Hansard*, 38th Parliament, 2nd Session, May 15, 2006.

43 *Residential Tenancies Act*, Section 53. According to the law, a landlord can raise a tenant's rent only by the annual rent increase guideline, if an allowable annual increase takes place during the period of the renovations.

44 Emily Mathieu, "Landlord Fined $75,000 for Evicting

Tenants in Bad Faith—Money It Can Recoup in Less Than a Year from Higher Rents," *Toronto Star*, February 24, 2019.

45 City of Toronto, *Eviction Prevention Handbook* (2021), 16.

46 City of Toronto, *Eviction Prevention Handbook*, 15. Later versions of the handbook continue to advise tenants to write their landlords about their intention to move back in after being evicted for renovations. See City of Toronto, *Preventing Evictions in Toronto* (2024), 24, 31.

TWO: THE LANDLORD PLAYBOOK

1 Other exceptions we know of are developer The Sud Group and corporate landlord Cromwell Management.

2 Susanne Soederberg, *Urban Displacements: Governing Surplus and Survival in Global Capitalism* (Abingdon, Oxon: Routledge, 2020), 50.

3 Landlords renovicting tenants will sometimes check off another reason on the notice, claiming they are either demolishing the unit or converting it to commercial use. What a landlord actually intends to do in a particular case can be hard to say. In our view, the reason checked off on an N13 notice does not determine whether or not renoviction is taking place.

4 Recently acquired buildings include those on Bansley Avenue and Torbolton and Leduc Drive in Toronto. Donovan Vincent, "Midtown Lowrise Tenants Band Together to Fight Renovation Evictions," *Toronto Star*, June 16, 2022; Angelyn Francis, "A New Landlord Ordered Them Out by End of March for Renovations: These Are Some of the People Who Are Staying Put," *Toronto Star*, March 23, 2021.

5 Joe McGinty and Taylor Pace, "'How Is This Legal?': Meet the King of Ontario Renovictions," *GuelphToday*, November 9, 2024; Gabe Oatley, "Tenants Facing Mass 'Renoviction' Take Protest to Forest Hill Home Owned by Elusive Company Director," *TorontoToday*, December 23, 2024.

6 In our experience, most tenants who receive N13 notices understand that their landlord is trying to permanently remove them from their homes. This is often obvious to tenants who are first approached informally with buyouts or N11 forms to end tenancies, or who are given N11 forms with their N13 notices. But tenants who receive N13s out of the blue or very soon after a sale may either take the claim on the notice at face value or be more receptive to bad advice.

7 Shane Dingman, "Landlord Warns Toronto Tenants Protest May Lead to Eviction," *Globe and Mail* (Toronto), October 19, 2022.

8 Matt Lundy, "Eviction Applications Spike in Ontario as Rents Soar, Vacancies Dwindle," *Globe and Mail* (Toronto), February 27, 2023.

9 Discussions that focus on the issue of landlords obtaining necessary permits similarly miss the mark. Landlords who renovict tenant routinely get permits and obtaining a permit is not difficult.

10 Emily Mathieu, "Tenants Say 'Flimsy' Law Opens Door to 'Renovictions,'" *Toronto Star*, March 23, 2018; Dingman, "Toronto City Councillor Warns of Eviction Notices Issued During Pandemic."

THREE: ORGANIZING AGAINST RENOVICTION

1 City of Toronto, *Eviction Prevention Handbook* (2021), 12; Bhavin Bilimoria and Karly Wilson, "Op-Ed: Advice to Tenants Facing Renoviction—Stay Put," *Now* (Toronto), January 12, 2022.

2 Canadian Centre for Housing Rights and National Right to Housing Network, *Implementing the Right to Housing in Canada: Renovations and Upgrading* (2022), 5.

3 Right to Housing Toronto, *Ending Homelessness & Preventing Evictions in Toronto: Rights Review* (2023), 16.

4 City of Toronto, *Preventing Evictions in Toronto* (2024).

5 ACORN Toronto, *Stop Renovictions in Toronto* (2021).
6 ACORN Toronto, *Stop Renovictions in Toronto*, 4.
7 Abby O'Brien, "These Toronto Tenants Stopped Their Entire Building from Being Evicted: Here's How They Did It," *CTV News*, April 22, 2022.
8 Fernando Arce, "Tenant Organizing Played Crucial Role in Stopping Renoviction," *Media Co-op*, August 26, 2023.
9 Parkdale Organize, "Parkdale Tenants Beat Renoviction," April 19, 2022, parkdaleorganize.ca.
10 Keele Area Tenant Committee, "About," keeletenants.wordpress.com; Parkdale Organize, "Statement of Principles," parkdaleorganize.ca.
11 Keele Area Tenant Committee, "Meeting Notes," November 7, 2022.
12 Lucy Villa, "Why I Joined the Keele Area Tenant Committee," Keele Area Tenant Newsletter, June 2025.
13 Keele Area Tenant Committee, "'Solidarity Means Togetherness': Tenants at 2960 Keele Stop Eviction," Keele Area Tenant Newsletter, February 2025.
14 Keele Area Tenant Committee, "'Don't Move Out. Come Together. Work Together,'" Keele Area Tenant Newsletter, June 2025.
15 Gabe Oatley, "Landlord-Tenant Mess: How a Multi-Year Ceiling Leak Spiralled into Assault Allegations, a Lost Job and Eviction Threats," *TorontoToday*, August 27, 2025.

FOUR: RENOVICTION AND THE STATE

1 Don Valley Community Legal Services, "Media Release: Time for Action on Renovictions," June 13, 2024.
2 Craig Heron, *The Canadian Labour Movement: A Short History* (Toronto: James Lorimer & Company Ltd., 2012); Jill Wade, "Wartime Housing Limited, 1941–1947: Canadian Housing Policy at the Crossroads," *Urban History Review* 15, no. 1 (1986): 40–59.

3 John Bacher, *Keeping to the Marketplace: The Evolution of Canadian Housing Policy* (Montreal: McGill-Queen's University Press, 1993).

4 Simon Clarke, *Keynesianism, Monetarism, and the Crisis of the State* (England: Edward Elgar Publishing Company Limited, 1988).

5 Bryan Palmer, *Canada's 1960s: The Ironies of Identity in a Rebellious Era* (Toronto: University of Toronto Press, 2009); Greg Suttor, *Still Renovating: A History of Canadian Social Housing Policy* (Montreal: McGill-Queen's University Press, 2016).

6 Peter Spurr, *Land and Urban Development: A Preliminary Study* (Toronto: James Lorimer & Company Ltd., 1976).

7 Agnoletto Stefano, *The Italians Who Built Toronto: Italian Workers and Contractors in the City's Housebuilding Industry, 1950–1980* (Oxford: Peter Lang Group AG, 2014).

8 Ontario Housing Corporation, "Memorandum on Labour Rates," October 8, 1965. P-10 M3-D (Metro Toronto–O.H. General File #5). Ontario Archive, Toronto, Ontario, Canada.

9 Clarke, *Keynesianism, Monetarism, and the Crisis of the State*, 345.

10 Douglas Hartle, *The Political Economy of Residential Rent Control in Ontario* (Toronto: Commission of Inquiry into Residential Tenancies, 1984).

11 Sean Purdy, "By the People, for the People: Tenant Organizing in Toronto's Regent Park Housing Project in the 1960s and 1970s," *Journal of Urban History* 30, no. 4 (2004): 519–48.

12 Jeffrey Jowell, "Landlord and Tenant Relations—Rent-Withholding in Ontario: A Case-Study and Suggestions for Legislation," *Canadian Bar Review* 48 (1970): 323–36; Mary Truemner and Bart Poesiat, "The West Lodge Files: Joining Clinic and Community to Overcome Tenants' Subordination," *Osgoode Hall Law Journal* 35, no. 3 (1997): 697–710.

13 W.T. Stanbury and Peter Thain, *The Origins of Rent Regulation in Ontario* (Toronto: Commission of Inquiry into Residential Tenancies, 1986).

14 Greg Albo, "Divided Province: Democracy and the Politics of State Restructuring in Ontario," in *Divided Province: Ontario Politics in the Age of Neoliberalism*, ed. Greg Albo and Bran Evans (Montreal: McGill-Queen's University Press, 2019); Steven High, *Industrial Sunset: The Making of North America's Rust Belt, 1969–1984* (Toronto: University of Toronto Press, 2003).

15 John Miron, "Private Rental Housing: The Canadian Experience," *Urban Studies* 32, no. 3 (1995): 579–604.

16 Doug Nesbitt, "Days of Action: Ontario's Extra-Parliamentary Opposition to the Common Sense Revolution, 1995–1998" (PhD diss., Queen's University, 2018), ProQuest (10969724).

17 Elinor Mahoney, "The Ontario Tenant Protection Act: A Trust Betrayed," *Journal of Law and Social Policy* 16, no. 1 (2001): 261–78.

18 Catherine Nash and Andrejs Skaburskis, "Toronto's Changing Rent Control Policy," in *Rent Control in North America and Four European Countries*, ed. William Smith and Michael Teitz (New York: Routledge, 1998).

19 Geoffrey Kay and James Mott, *Political Order and the Law of Labor* (London: Macmillan, 1982), 96.

20 City of Toronto, "Promoting the Security of Residential Rental Tenancies," November 5, 2019, toronto.ca.

21 City of Toronto, *Preventing Evictions in Toronto* (2024), 24–26.

22 Samantha Beattie, "Hamilton to Become 1st Ontario City with Bylaw to Stop 'Bad Faith' Renovictions," *CBC News*, January 18, 2024.

23 Nevertheless, when advocates pushed the City of Toronto to adopt a Hamilton-style bylaw, councillor Paula Fletcher

demonstrated her poor understanding of the issue when she said, "The key to stopping a renoviction is the building permit. Often, landlords give tenants an N13 and . . . they never get a building permit. They never do the renovations." Ryan Jones, "Could Hamilton's Anti-Renoviction Bylaw Work in Toronto?: Council Committee Wants to Find Out," *CBC News*, February 28, 2024.

24 Lane Harrison, "Demovictions Are on the Rise in Toronto: Some Fear They'll Make the Rental Market Worse for Everyone," *CBC News*, October 3, 2023.

25 City of Toronto, "Implementing a Rental Renovation Licence Bylaw to Address Renovictions," October 16, 2024, toronto.ca; Shawn Jeffords, "Key Toronto Committee Endorses Plan to Prevent Renovictions," *CBC News*, June 16, 2024.

26 City of Toronto, "Implementing a Rental Renovation Licence Bylaw to Address Renovictions"; City of Toronto, "Rental Renovation Licence Bylaw," available at: toronto.ca.

27 Dilshad Burman, "'We Have Been Heard': Advocates Laud Toronto's Renoviction Bylaw Framework," *City News*, October 23, 2024.

28 Samantha Beattie, "Hamilton Tenants Without Running Water for 8 Weeks Remain Stuck in 'Horrendous' Situation, Says Councillor," *CBC News*, February 23, 2023.

29 Justin Chandler, "Last 2 Tenants in a Gutted Hamilton Apartment Building Are Left Without Heat," *CBC News*, December 24, 2023.

30 Manuela Vega, "Toronto Fire Ordered Their Landlords to Comply with the Fire Code: Now, These Tenants Fear Losing Their Affordable Rentals for Good," *Toronto Star*, May 20, 2025.

31 Lane Harrison, "Should Demovicting Developers Have to Double New Rentals?: One Toronto Councillor Thinks So," *CBC News*, October 12, 2023.

32 Susanne Soederberg, *Urban Displacements: Governing*

Surplus and Survival in Global Capitalism (Abingdon, Oxon: Routledge, 2020), 50.

33 Geoffrey Kay and James Mott, *Political Order and the Law of Labor* (London: Macmillan, 1982), 148.

34 Liam Casey, "Ontario to Beef Up Tenant Protections, Prevent Renovictions, Housing Minister Says," *Canadian Press*, April 5, 2023.

35 Nicola Seguin, "Halifax Real Estate Listings Advertising Fixed-Term Leases as Financial Asset for Buyers," *CBC News*, June 4, 2025.

36 Kerry Campbell, "P.E.I. Declares Moratorium on 'Renovictions' for 2 Years," *CBC News*, November 17, 2021.

37 Arturo Chang, "With 'Renovictions' Moratorium Set to Expire, Advocates Say New Protections Not Enough," *CBC News*, October 23, 2023.

38 Matthew Lapierre and Erika Morris, "No More Lease Transfers?: Quebec Has Passed a New Housing Law; Here's What's in It," *CBC News*, February 22, 2024.

39 Erika Morris, "Quebec Bill Banning Certain Evictions Passed into Law," *CBC News*, June 6, 2024.

40 Savannah Stewart, "How an 'Explosion' of Renovictions Have Been Left Unchecked in Quebec," *Ricochet*, June 26, 2023.

41 Rob Hunter, "The Capitalist State as a Historically Specific Social Form," in *Marxism and the Capitalist State: Towards a New Debate*, ed. Rob Hunter, Rafael Khachaturian, and Eva Nanopoulos (Cham, Switzerland: Palgrave Macmillan, 2023): 253–74.

42 Dilshad Burman, "Multiple Lankin Investments Building Tenants Protest Above Guideline Rent Increase," *City News*, April 15, 2025.

43 Shannon Carranco, "Parkdale Tenants Rally Against Goliath Corporate Landlords," *The Hoser*, March 29, 2021.

44 Andrew Crosby, *Resisting Eviction: Domicide and*

the Financialization of Rental Housing (Halifax: Fernwood, 2023), 107.

45 Neal Rockwell, "In a Toronto Neighbourhood, Renters Go Up Against Big Owners," *Al Jazeera*, December 6, 2023.

46 Fernando Acre, "LTB Sides with Landlord to Expedite AGI Hearings, Blindsides Tenants," *The Hoser*, August 29, 2023.

47 Simon Clarke, "State, Class Struggle, and the Reproduction of Capital," in *The State Debate*, ed. Simon Clarke (London: Macmillan, 1991): 183–201.

48 Ricardo Tranjan, *The Tenant Class* (Toronto: Between the Lines, 2023).

49 Tracy Rosenthal and Leonardo Vilchis, *Abolish Rent: How Tenants Can End the Housing Crisis* (LaVergne: Haymarket Books, 2024), 121.

50 Nick Bano, *Against Landlords: How to Solve the Housing Crisis* (London: Verso, 2024).

CONCLUSION

1 Jenna Benchetrit, "Bank of Canada Makes Another Hefty Rate Cut with Slower Pace of Cuts Going Forward," *CBC News*, December 11, 2024.

2 CMHC, "2025 Mid-Year Rental Market Update," July 8, 2025.

3 Andrew Oliphant, "Hamilton Tenants Take Ownership of Their Building and Run It as a Cooperative," *Media Co-op*, June 20, 2025.

COLE WEBBER is a community legal worker at Parkdale Community Legal Services in Toronto.

PHILIP ZIGMAN is a co-creator of RenovictionsTO.